THE PROMPT HERO METHOD

HOW BUSINESS PROFESSIONALS GET EXECUTIVE-LEVEL RESULTS FROM **GPT, GEMINI, CLAUDE OR ANY AI** WITHOUT WRITING CODE

NARCISO SILVA

Questions? publishing@synecticstudio.com

TABLE OF CONTENTS

Your Free Prompt Hero Toolkit

This book is designed to be a complete, self-contained resource. Everything you need to master advanced prompting is in the chapters ahead. To help you go even further, I've created **four free companion resources** that extend your learning and help you apply what you read even faster. I'd encourage you to grab them now so they're ready when you need them.

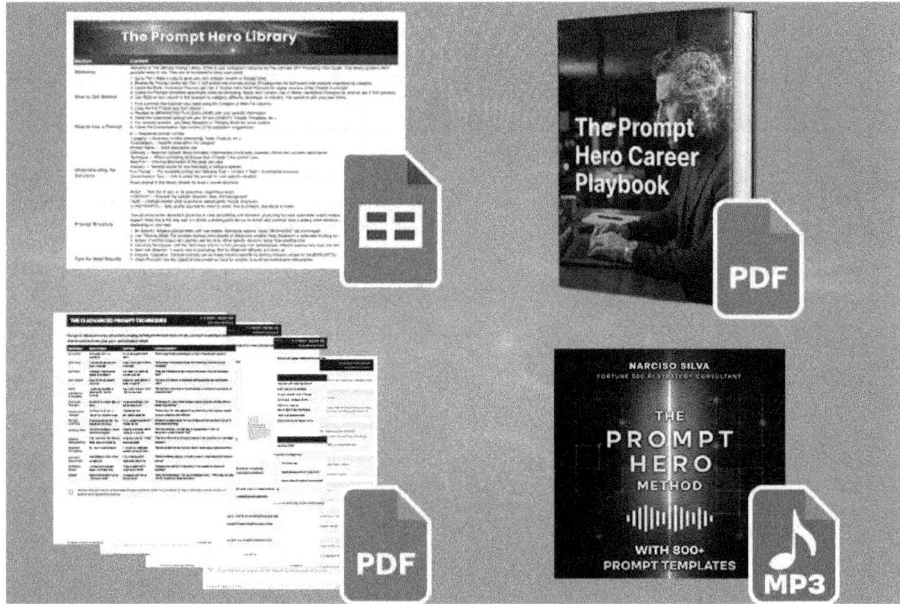

Sign up for free and get:

- **800+ ready-to-use business prompts library** organized by function, industry, and technique. For the days when you know what you need but can't find the right words, this library gives you a proven starting point in seconds instead of a blank screen.

- **Prompting for Career Growth, a 15,000-word standalone guide** with a complete system for turning your prompt skills into career advancement, from landing interviews to earning promotions.
- **The Reference Guides:** A set of cheat sheets with all the main topics of the book summarized for quick reference
- **The Audiobook:** so you can listen to the concepts of the book from anywhere.

You already invested in learning the method. These bonuses make sure you get the most out of it. **Free. Ten seconds. Scan the QR code or visit the link below.**

https://synecticpublishing.kit.com/7ba6afb204

Feedback or questions? Please drop me a line here:
publishing@synecticstudio.com

INTRODUCTION

Goldman Sachs estimates that artificial intelligence (AI) could automate up to 25% of all professional tasks globally and unlock nearly $7 trillion in global economic value in the next decade (*Generative AI*, 2023). McKinsey reports that knowledge workers who adopt AI effectively can see productivity gains of between 30% and 60% (Chui et al., 2023). If you've seen similar headlines on the effectiveness of AI, you've probably tried asking ChatGPT or an equivalent large language model (LLM) to draft a market entry strategy, write an email, or even analyze a financial report with the hope that it might jump-start your thinking. However, the output was probably the same disappointing, generic, surface-level summaries everyone gets.

On the other hand, you see your peers quietly accelerating past you. Leaders who suddenly deliver strategies in half the time, analysts who produce insight-rich reports in minutes, and entrepreneurs who launch new product lines seemingly overnight. Despite your experience, intelligence, and willingness to experiment with technology, you aren't getting those kinds of results. You've tried different prompts, applied the tips you found online, and even skimmed the "Top 10 Prompts for Professionals" articles flooding your LinkedIn feed. Regardless of all these efforts, the outputs don't match the quality or sophistication required for high-stakes decisions. At this point, you're probably wondering, *What am I missing*?

Allow me to ease your mind. What you and a thousand other professionals feel is far from a lack of potential (on your part) but rather a slight communication problem. While AI is an incredible tool that's capable of extraordinary performance, without clear instructions, it performs suboptimally. Unlocking real business acumen from an AI model requires more than casual experimentation or endless copy-and-paste prompt lists. It takes understanding how AI translates user queries and context into usable, quality outputs.

It's important to discern that when tasks become more complex, sensitive, or strategic, basic AI prompts feel shallow and often miss the mark. I've realized that most leaders use AI like an intern, yet when handled properly, it can operate like a chief strategy officer, head of research and development, senior market analyst, or innovation partner. The reason for this is that most professionals have never been taught how to communicate with an AI system at the level required for top-tier performance.

I'm not referring to simple commands such as "Write this email," "Summarize this document," or "Give me five ideas," although these can be effective instructional prompts. As I extrapolate in Chapter 1, I'm talking about structured, context-rich, business-grade prompting designed to interface with the model's reasoning systems: the level of prompting that transforms the model from a text generator into a strategic asset capable of analysis, scenario planning, product ideation, systems design, risk evaluation, market intelligence gathering, and operational optimization. I'm referring to advanced prompting that can remove weeks from strategic cycles and produce insights that would otherwise take days of labor by human teams and a chunky bite out of your budget.

Here's my observation from working with leadership cohorts integrating AI in their operations: Professionals today face two major interconnected challenges that obstruct their mastery of this technology. The first is what I call the "professional gap." This is the barrier between AI's capabilities and the practical guidance available for integrating it into complex, high-pressure workflows. For instance, you're expected to make high-stakes decisions, communicate with precision, and produce work that shapes revenue, risk, and reputation. You can't rely on simplistic prompts or generic frameworks. Instead, you need advanced techniques that can easily be adapted to the realities of your industry, your team, and your strategic objectives. Unfortunately, these techniques don't appear in viral social media posts or beginner-friendly AI courses.

The second challenge is the shortage of deeply informed, niche-specific prompting guidance. The reason behind this content deficit is that mainstream literature and overhyped digital guides focus on entertaining tricks or shallow use cases because they're easy to teach and easy to sell. Very little material explains how to think with an LLM, how to structure multilayered instructions that shape the model's reasoning, or how to guide it through complex domain-specific processes. Even fewer resources show you how to build repeatable, high-performance prompt systems capable of producing consistent and reliable output.

I'm thrilled to announce that this book exists to solve these problems and set you apart as a technology expert, with proven methods that will transform you into an AI-powered superhero through advanced prompting.

With over 20 years of experience as a Big 3 AI strategy consultant guiding Fortune 500 executives through digital transformation, I've helped organizations not only embrace AI but also cut through the noise and use it as a growth engine.

I've worked directly with companies that had brilliant ideas but couldn't scale them because their teams were relying on basic prompting. Once they adopted structured, advanced methods, they unlocked previously unattainable results: detailed product launch strategies produced in a single session; competitor intelligence generated through multistep analytical modeling; validated revenue opportunities discovered through scenario-based reasoning; and personalized, high-performing marketing assets that outpaced human benchmarks.

Similarly, once you understand the AI prompting mechanics within this book, you'll gain a strategic advantage that compounds across every part of your professional life. You'll produce deeper insights faster, make clearer decisions with richer data, and accelerate execution and innovation like never before. You'll reduce cognitive load while increasing the quality of your thinking. Most importantly, you'll position yourself on the right side of the technological segregation that's rapidly separating future-ready leaders from those who'll struggle to remain competitive.

If you're wondering about my confidence to make such audacious claims, let me allay your fears. My methodology is built on thousands of hours of experimentation, cross-industry consulting, and hands-on refinement. I've authored two best-selling books in this series that have helped thousands of professionals adopt AI fundamentals. If you're interacting with my work for the first time, feel free to grab copies of *The Ultimate Guide to Mastering AI for Leaders* and *The Ultimate Guide to AI Agents for Business Leaders and Entrepreneurs*. If you're a returning reader, your loyalty doesn't go unnoticed. Thank you!

This book goes further to distill the advanced prompting strategies I've used with leaders in finance, manufacturing, software as a service (SaaS), consulting, marketing, and enterprise operations. The frameworks inside are designed to be immediately usable, reliably repeatable, and adaptable to any professional context.

You'll learn to think like an AI model and guide its reasoning with precision. You'll also learn how to use these techniques to generate executive-level deliverables in a fraction of the usual time. Furthermore, you'll gain access to a wide-ranging library of high-performance prompt templates specifically engineered for strategic planning, innovation, analysis, communication, market intelligence, ops optimization, and more. You can jump ahead to Chapter 8 for a sneak peek at the prompt library before coming back to Chapters 1–3 for a deep dive on advanced prompt techniques.

If you're ready to stop getting generic answers and instead turn AI into a competitive advantage that accelerates your career, strengthens your business, and transforms how you solve problems, you've found the guide you need. This book will teach you how to command AI with clarity, structure, and strategic intent. The goal is to help you unlock a level of performance previously accessible only to those who understand prompt engineering at the highest level, without arduous years of study! I'll see you inside :)

CHAPTER

1

INTRODUCTION TO GENERATIVE AI PROMPT MASTERY

The latest McKinsey survey on the state of AI reveals that while 80% of professionals and organizations are now using AI in their operations, the degree of adoption remains in the pilot phase (Singla et al., 2025). This indicates the existence of a wide gap between those who are embracing AI and those who are seeing major results from integrating it. Becoming an AI-powered tech hero requires more than understanding the basics or using AI like a search engine. It involves harnessing this technology fully and mastering how to give AI clear instructions to yield top-tier results.

To begin with, understanding AI's core structure and building blocks is essential for results-driven implementation. For this reason, this chapter levels the playing field and demystifies the jargon you'll encounter in this book so that no meaning is lost to technicality. It also provides foundational knowledge about how generative AI works, the significance of prompting, different prompt types, and techniques that unlock high-quality results.

AI Building Blocks

AI recently took center stage as the most widely adopted technology, surpassing crypto, social media, and the internet combined. However, it's not such a new concept as most people think. History reveals that AI dates as far back as the 1950s, emerging from the "Turing test," where Alan Turing questioned a machine's ability to think or demonstrate human-like intelligence (Epstein, 1992). This involved tests that measured computer systems' ability to imitate human conversations such that it wasn't possible to distinguish machine-generated from human-created responses. While this significant test revealed shortcomings such as the computers' finite understanding of linguistics and syntax, it set the foundation for the AI we know today. I'm assuming you know "AI" as a broad umbrella term that describes a system's ability to perform tasks that typically require human intelligence, like decision-making, pattern recognition, communication, reasoning, and problem-solving.

From an executive lens, we need to see AI not as "machines thinking" but as machines predicting the most statistically likely outcome given the data they've seen. This narrative derives from the three pillars that fundamentally power AI: data, models, and algorithms. You can think of data as the machine's experience, or what it processes from the input in order to output information. AI models are the brains of the system and the term I'll be using to refer to any AI tool. Algorithms are the logic and rules governing the behavior of these models. Therefore, AI systems don't think; they process the data they've been fed and learn from it to predict (generate) new information based on user queries (prompts).

Most of what organizations call AI today is built on machine learning (also known as ML) and deep learning (or DL).

Machine Learning

Machine learning is an AI branch that refers to a system's ability to learn from historical data through rigorous training instead of hard programming. For example, if you feed a system enough examples, it starts recognizing patterns and predicting what comes next. A common machine learning example is showing an AI model a bunch of object pictures (dogs, cats, pizza, apples, etc.) and labeling them, after which the model uses image recognition abilities to distinguish a specific object the next time it sees it. Similarly, models are trained to predict text and sentiments using large text datasets that use natural language.

Essentially, if traditional software is rule-based ("If X happens, do Y"), machine learning is pattern-based ("If you've seen this pattern before, here's the likely next step"). If you were to build your own AI model specific to your industry or expertise, you'd need to train it with relevant data that it could then use to predict and generate outcomes based on the given instructions. Let's say your training data included lead generation strategies; your AI models would easily answer prompts about predicting customer churn and lead conversion and even suggest the next possible course of action to retain customers. Fortunately, you don't have to train your own AI models because the existing ones are already trained with extensive amounts of data. However, effective prompting enables you to extract data that's more relevant to your industry to solve your problems.

Deep Learning

Deep learning is a subset of machine learning that uses layers of interconnected information transmitters, also known as "neural networks," inspired by the human brain. This enables AI to go deeper than predicting next tokens based on historical training data through the ability to self-improve via multiple layers of data processing. Deep learning's strength is evident in its ability to detect non-obvious patterns across massive datasets, from images to text, speech, anomalies, or customer signals. If you've ever wondered how Netflix can recommend the next binge-worthy show, the clue is deep learning. It learns from your historic viewing patterns and goes the extra mile to learn and suggest related content.

Deep learning unlocked the last decade of breakthrough technology, as seen in mobile facial recognition, voice assistants like Siri and Alexa, self-driving cars, medical image diagnostics, and, ultimately, generative AI. PwC (2025) predicted that AI could contribute up to $15.7 trillion to the global economy by 2030, with the largest portion of that value coming from generative AI's ability to generate content and make decisions that previously required expensive human talent. This is precisely why organizations and leaders must understand AI prompting.

Understanding Generative AI

As the name suggests, generative AI is a type of AI that can generate new content in any modality (text, code, images, audio, or video) based on training data and the instructions (prompts) it's given. In essence, generative AI is trained on large datasets to help it recognize patterns that give it the ability to perform human-inspired tasks. Just as you're able to learn, think, analyze, and develop ideas from common sense, generative AI can create content based on prompts without explicit programming.

Before OpenAI released its first Generative Pre-trained Transformer (GPT-1) in 2018 (Lacy, 2024), the term "generative" was used loosely with little consideration of what it entailed. Generative AI gained traction from late 2022 following the public release of ChatGPT, OpenAI's interactive chatbot, which reached 100 million users in less than 2 months and has since become a household name (Curry, 2026).

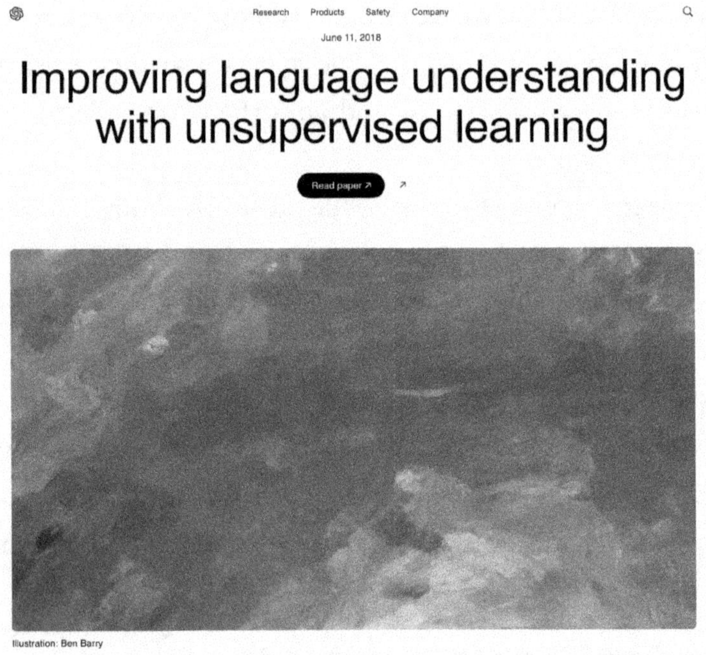

One of the best ways to understand generative AI is to compare it to other types of AI, such as traditional AI. Traditional AI performs tasks strictly based on existing data or within set parameters. For instance, traditional AI can analyze and classify given data and make predictions or decisions within certain boundaries, while generative AI can create something completely new.

Think of a spam filter analyzing emails from a suspicious sender versus an email autoresponder. The former has limited tasks, such as simply identifying spam emails from unverified addresses and categorizing them (not deleting them), while the latter has the ability to read the email and formulate and send a sensible response.

We can also differentiate generative AI from agentic AI, which is currently making strides. Agentic AI merges the capabilities of both generative and traditional AI in that it works within a predefined workflow automation to carry out generative tasks like a human agent would; however, it doesn't stop at generating new content but multitasks and goes on to make decisions based on real-time conditions. For full context, I've devoted an entire book to agentic AI for business leaders and entrepreneurs, available on Amazon.

Examples of generative AI include LLMs such as ChatGPT and Google Gemini, image generators like Midjourney and DALL·E, and conversational generative chatbots. All these AI models can generate new content in real time through machine learning, deep learning, and natural language processing (NLP). NLP is a branch of AI that merges machine learning with computational linguistics to enable machines to understand and process language the way humans do (through text and speech). It underpins simplified (non-technical) communication between the user and the system, which plays a pivotal role in generative AI. In the past, a lack of advanced computer literacy and coding skills limited non-technical people from instructing machines to perform tasks. NLP and prompt engineering bridge that gap today; the quality of AI-generated content now depends on your communication skills, which anyone can enhance.

Prompt Mastery

A prompt is a query you input into any AI, LLM, or GPT model to get a useful response. You might ask yourself why prompting matters. While anyone can use AI in their business, only those who master prompting get the desired executive-grade results. How you communicate with AI determines whether it gives you a competitive advantage or remains an underutilized tool. A prompt is the foundation and primary guide that tells a model what to do, how to do it, in what style, at what depth, for which audience, and with what considerations.

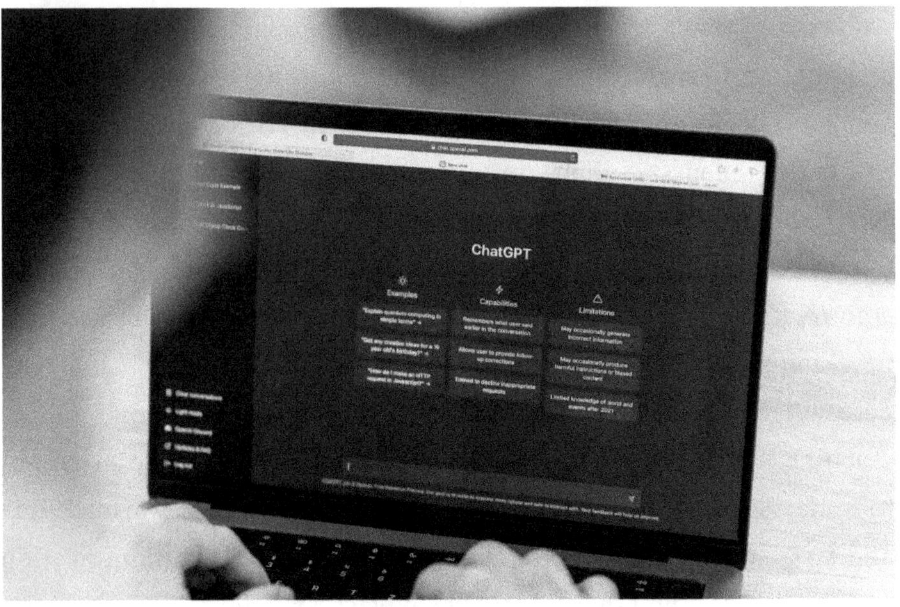

Like in any communicative setting, articulating your thoughts in an unconfusing manner enables AI to come up with helpful solutions and follow instructions fully. A clear and well-structured prompt shapes the output quality and the model's overall helpfulness, while a vague prompt yields generic and suboptimal output. My goal is to help you advance from getting basic responses to obtaining effective results that give you a competitive edge in your sphere of influence. It all starts with understanding different prompt design principles, types, and life cycles.

Core Prompt Design Principles

Clarity

A clear prompt ensures that the AI understands what you want and how you want it delivered. You shouldn't let it guess its task if you want top-tier results. Always state your objective, formatting, and expectations clearly to help the AI understand the task quickly without any confusion. For example, "Write a 200-word summary of the business book *Lean Startup* by Eric Ries. Use professional language, and structure the summary into three sections: introduction, key strategies, and practical applications."

Specificity

Ambiguity produces generic and off-topic responses. Therefore, narrow an AI model's focus by detailing what you want and what you don't want, and mention relevant constraints or parameters to work within. Specify the tone, perspective, length, and expertise level to ensure that your prompt gets the desired results.

For example, when using AI to create a business plan, clearly specify your target market, revenue goals, and competitive advantages: "Write a marketing strategy focused on digital channels for a sustainable fashion start-up targeting eco-conscious millennials, with a professional yet approachable tone, a length of 1,000 words, and insights suitable for early-stage entrepreneurs." Specificity guides the model to avoid generic advice on marketing or unrelated industries so you receive precise, actionable guidance.

Context

Context provides a little bit of background for a model to adhere to when carrying out a task. Bear in mind that an LLM doesn't inherently know your business environment, personality, or audience. Therefore, giving it enough context can improve output relevance drastically.

For example, "You're a senior marketing executive preparing a presentation for the board of directors. Your audience is highly knowledgeable about industry trends and company performance. The goal is to clearly communicate the current market position, highlight strategic initiatives, and propose actionable recommendations to drive growth in the upcoming fiscal year. Use formal language, focus on data-driven insights, and be concise yet persuasive."

Brevity

Conciseness is key to clear instructions. Be specific, and provide enough context without being too verbose. Don't be too repetitive, and use fewer words to make your prompt less confusing. For example, "Summarize this quarterly sales report, highlighting key trends and action points in 150 words or less."

Relevance

A relevant prompt is pertinent to the task at hand and doesn't contain any useless details beyond the subject matter. Giving AI extra details can dilute your instruction and output quality, as it often considers everything in the prompt to give a comprehensive response. Guide the output quality by sharing relevant details only. For example, "Analyze the quarterly sales data for our North American division, identify key factors driving revenue growth, and suggest actionable strategies to improve underperforming product lines."

Open-Endedness vs. Closed-Endedness

Open-ended prompts encourage expansive, creative, and elaborative responses without strict limits, allowing for personal interpretation and detailed answers. Closed-ended prompts, on the other hand, seek specific, concise answers (often yes/no or one-word responses), limiting the scope of the reply. For example, "What are your thoughts on the impact of AI in modern education?" (open-ended) vs. "Is technology important in education? Yes or no?" (closed-ended).

Positivity

Framing prompts positively can encourage constructive and optimistic responses. Asking how effective AI integration is in your profession will yield a more supportive response than asking how ineffective or dangerous it might be. Positive wording helps create an engaging, supportive tone for interaction and task alignment. For example, "How can AI integration enhance efficiency and innovation in business operations?" vs. "What are the dangers of integrating AI in a start-up's business operations?"

Iterative Refinement

Iterative refinement means adjusting and fine-tuning your prompt based on feedback and results to improve effectiveness. Sometimes, the initial prompt provides a subpar output or one that doesn't answer the query satisfactorily. Unlike with a search engine, where you'd need to run a new search, AI leaves room for improvement as models consider the initial prompts and incorporate the latest query into the final response. You can start with a vague prompt and refine it multiple times until you get the desired quality based on the output feedback. This prompt design is often improved through cycles of testing and refinement, as shown in the example process for generating a marketing email below:

1. **Initial prompt:** "Write a marketing email to promote a new software product."
2. **First refinement (based on output feedback: this is too generic):** "Write a marketing email to small business owners

promoting our new project management software that helps teams collaborate efficiently."

3. **Second refinement (based on output feedback: needs a more persuasive tone and a clear call to action):** "Write a persuasive marketing email targeting small business owners promoting our new project management software that boosts team collaboration and productivity. Include a special 20% discount offer and a clear call to action to sign up for a free trial."
4. **Third refinement (based on output feedback: add benefits and a customer testimonial):** "Write a persuasive, friendly marketing email targeting small business owners promoting our new project management software that boosts team collaboration and productivity. Highlight benefits like time-saving automation, easy task tracking, and improved communication. Include a customer testimonial and a clear call to action to sign up for a free 14-day trial with a 20% discount."

CORE PRINCIPLES OF PROMPT DESIGN

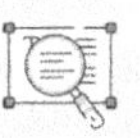

Clarity
State your objective, structure, and expectations so the AI knows exactly what you want.

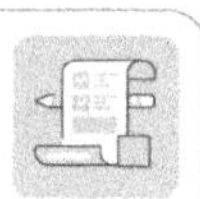

Specificity
Define parameters and constraints to avoid generic responses using scope, tone, format, and style.

Context
Provide relevant background so the AI tailors responses to your audience and situation.

Brevity
Be concise with enough detail to guide, but no repetition or unnecessary length.

Relevance
Share only details that directly pertain to your goal and omit unrelated information.

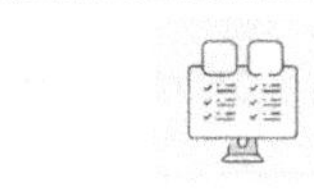

Open vs. Closed-Endedness
Choose between broad, creative responses or specific, constrained answers as needed.

Positivity
Frame prompts constructively to drive supportive, solution-focused outputs.

Iterative Refinement
Improve prompts through feedback cycles: test, evaluate, and refine until the output matches your goal.

Common Types of Prompts

Instructional Prompts

An instructional prompt is a clear and direct command that tells an AI model exactly what to do using verbs such as "write," "summarize," "list," or "compare." If you want a lengthy report summarized into a paragraph or five main bullet points, simply instruct the AI, and it will respond accordingly. An explicit command, such as "Summarize this article in one paragraph," "List ten leadership steps to motivate my team," or "Generate a caption for this image," ensures that the model doesn't have to figure out the output but instead can simply follow instructions. Instructional prompts can be used for standard operating procedures (SOPs), task workflows, email drafting, report writing, or content generation.

Question-Based Prompts

Some queries request explanations, insights, or specific knowledge, and framing a prompt as a question enables AI to research or think before answering. For example, "What are the main risks of entering the West African fintech market?" "How is AI reshaping the workforce globally?" "Which business sectors are still facing post-pandemic crises?" Question-based prompts are more effective with queries that require the AI to go through multiple sources to generate a comprehensive response. Asking AI models probing questions can help you with detailed research, due diligence, and strategy development without having to manually go through various information sources.

Role-Based Prompts

When you need expert judgment or authority-aligned communication, instruct the model to adopt a clear role or persona—CFO, regulator, skeptical customer, or industry analyst—and require it to reason from that viewpoint. Assigning the AI a persona, expertise, or perspective can yield game-changing results when prompting. Instead of returning a generic or safe response, the model gets into character, evaluates all relevant aspects, and responds according to the specified role. For instance, rather than simply asking AI to edit a piece of writing, consider this role-based prompt: "You're a meticulous *Harvard Business Review* copy editor; proofread this SEO article for clarity and coherence, remove redundancy, spelling, and grammar errors, and provide suggestions for polished copy."

If you ask the AI to act as an authority addressing a specific audience, it amplifies the tone and expertise level and returns industry-level output. You might get more from the prompt "Act as a CEO coach and critique this leadership communication style" than if you simply ask if a style is okay or not. Role-based prompts can be useful in expert consultations, simulations, or advisory support.

Creative Prompts

Creative prompts encourage AI to be imaginative, think divergently, and create something original. This is where generative AI becomes an absolute paradigm shift toward limitless possibilities. AI can create beyond limits; therefore, giving it an imaginative, creative prompt often yields results with the "wow factor." For example, "Generate five innovative product ideas for busy entrepreneurs." "Design a minimalistic, abstract, geometric, or clean logo using the following palette." "Write a compelling product description." Creative prompts can elevate your branding, ideation, marketing, and product innovation.

Analytical Prompts

One of the best ways to use AI at an executive level is to help you evaluate, compare, or analyze data or ideas. Even if you don't really understand or even like reading graphs or charts, asking AI to interpret complex data can save you time on time-sensitive tasks where you need to make informed decisions. For example, if you need to go through customer insights or compare products based on market performance, AI can help sift through a ton of metrics and reviews, assess key performance indicators (KPIs), and give you comprehensive feedback instantly. A highly effective analytical prompt would be "Analyze customer feedback and extract key sentiment patterns" or "Compare our website click-through rates from Q2 to Q3 and indicate which landing page has had the highest lead conversion."

Conversational Prompts

Sometimes, the first prompt yields an output that requires a follow-up prompt or a number of multi-turn conversations before you're satisfied. Conversational prompts sustain an open, free-flowing dialogue to iterate your ideas or queries until the output is on point. AI models are designed to be flexible; as such, they allow users to change their queries, perspective, and rules and reframe their prompts until they're satisfied with the output. You can use conversational prompts to prepare for an interview, brainstorming, coaching session, or any ongoing project research.

For instance, you can say, "Tell me more about the challenges small teams face when scaling," and follow up with "How do successful organizations overcome these challenges?" You can then further refine: "Ignore the first two challenges because they don't apply to my company size. Replace them with relevant ones, and suggest ways to overcome them, considering the scaling goals I shared earlier." These prompts aren't just one command that yields a simple response; instead, they demonstrate a back-and-forth conversation with an AI model where you refine your prompts while the model considers previous prompts and incorporates your latest query in the final output.

Contextual Prompts

Contextual prompts provide useful background details along with the query to guide the relevance and accuracy of the model's output. As I mentioned earlier, providing context helps you avoid getting generic output, as the model considers all the given (explicit) and implied (implicit) intents to give a more targeted response. For example, "You're helping a B2B SaaS start-up with 12 employees and $40k MRR. Our main goal is to reduce churn. Given this context, recommend top priorities." This prompt yields a more tailored response than if you simply asked for "Five churn reduction strategies." Contextual prompts can be effective for strategy sessions, scenario planning, tailored insights, or any queries where background information alignment is key.

Step-by-Step Prompts

A step-by-step prompt is a structured query that involves a sequential breakdown, where a model reveals its chain of thought leading toward the final answer. For example, "Give me a step-by-step plan for launching a digital product in 30 days." This prompt is an explicit instruction to the AI model, indicating that you want a well-thought-out output from start to finish. The response will indicate the requested steps and format them neatly into periods and tasks, such as "Day 1: Product Ideation and Validation (review the concept and target audience), Day 2: Demand (market research)... Day 20: Pre-Launch Marketing... Day 29: Final Testing, and Day 30: Launch Day (Go live with your product)."

A step-by-step prompt guides the model to think out loud, show reasoning, and highlight any important milestones needed to complete a task. You can use this prompt when performing tasks that involve multiple processes, such as creating a product, developing a recipe, writing a book, or documenting a process. You need a list of ingredients, time, instructions, and cooking method for a recipe, or a title, subtitle, outline, and chapter breakdown before filling the pages of a book with content.

Prompt type	**When to use**
Instructional	When you need clear, direct commands for tasks like summarizing, listing, drafting emails, or creating content
Question-based	When seeking explanations, insights, or detailed responses from multiple sources for research or strategy
Role-based	When requiring expert judgment or authoritative, persona-driven communication, such as editing or critiques
Creative	When encouraging imaginative, original creation, like innovative ideas, designs, or compelling descriptions
Analytical	When analyzing, comparing, or evaluating data, metrics, or insights for informed decision-making
Conversational	When engaging in multi-turn dialogues to refine ideas or queries, such as brainstorming or ongoing projects
Contextual	When background information is essential to tailor responses to specific scenarios or business contexts
Step-by-step	When tasks need a sequential breakdown or a detailed framework, such as product launches, recipes, or plans

The Prompt Life Cycle

1. **Planning and design:** Before a prompt is even drafted, careful planning is necessary. This is the brainstorming phase, where the prompt's purpose, target audience, and key performance metrics are outlined. It also includes identifying the ideal AI model or platform for the task.
2. **Creation:** The initial prompt generation means setting a clear task definition and giving an AI model instructions or something to work on. It requires understanding the objective and designing a prompt in a way that guides the model toward generating the desired outcome. This developmental stage also includes adding context and background information, as well as incorporating all requirements identified in the planning stage. You can create an appropriate prompt by selecting from the types listed above.
3. **Testing:** In this phase, the created prompt is used in real or simulated scenarios to observe how it performs. Testing helps identify whether the prompt generates relevant and useful responses. It also ensures that prompts are reliable, helpful, and harmless before being released for deployment (published or integrated into your system).
4. **Evaluation:** After testing, the results are closely examined to assess the prompt's effectiveness. Metrics or qualitative analysis can be used to determine if the prompt meets the intended goals.
5. **Refinement:** Based on the evaluation results, prompts are optimized and improved. This phase involves tweaking a few sections, rewording, adding specificity and clarity, removing redundancy, and retesting for optimal performance. It determines readiness for prompt execution.

6. **Deployment:** Once optimization is done and all improvements are in place, the prompt is activated in the intended environment, whether it's integrated into a system, shared with other users, or published.

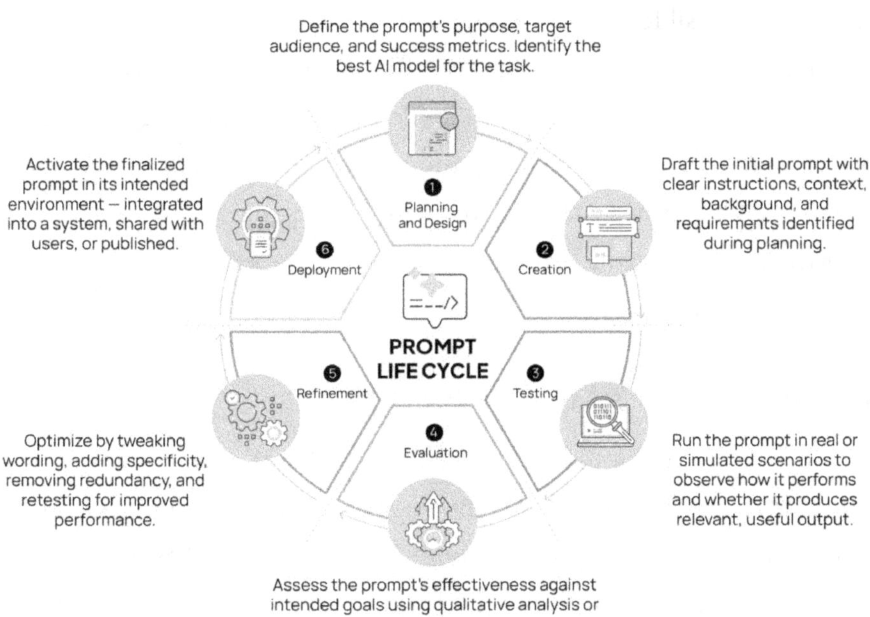

Common Pitfalls and Quick Solutions

The machine's intelligence depends on the user's direction; as the saying goes, "Garbage in equals garbage out." Just as you can expect some errors when working with humans, AI isn't perfect either. However, there are common mistakes that you as the user should avoid to minimize using AI ineffectively. This section also provides quick solutions to incorporate into your AI integration to maximize quality outputs.

Vagueness

We've already established the importance of specificity when prompting AI models. To reiterate, ensure that you give clear, unconfusing, and specific instructions. Don't let an AI figure out the details you want by itself. While most LLMs can understand your implicit intent, be as explicit as possible to avoid vague and generic responses.

For example, "Create a marketing strategy for our company" is vague compared to "Develop a detailed digital marketing strategy for our mid-sized ecommerce company specializing in eco-friendly home products. The strategy should focus on increasing online sales by 25% over the next 6 months through targeted social media campaigns, email marketing, and influencer partnerships."

Too Many Queries in One Prompt

While I said you should include as much detail and context in your prompts as possible, it's important to structure your prompts in a way that an LLM finds easy to tackle. If you bombard AI with too many questions, it might end up rambling, hallucinating, and giving you suboptimal results. You can start with one or a few (relatable) questions and refine the prompt as you follow up.

For instance, "What are the current market trends for renewable energy? Can you list major competitors and their market shares? Also, what are the best marketing strategies for a new solar panel company? And how should we price our product compared to competitors?" This is too busy and confusing for the model. The improved version could be more focused and structured, in the following manner: "What are the current market trends for renewable energy, particularly solar panels? After that, please help me identify major competitors and their market share." Then, in follow-up prompts, you could ask about marketing strategies and pricing.

Embedding New Queries Into Chat History

In most cases, an LLM will open the last session you had instead of directing you to a new chat because of its built-in memory. Previous chats can contribute to the model's confusion or biased responses. Unless you're following up on a project, it's recommended that you delete your chat history before starting a new query. For example, before asking about "Q2 sales strategy optimization," clear the chat history so the model can generate targeted, unbiased recommendations based solely on your current business goals. This allows the model to give fresh output based on the specific prompt without blending in prior (often unrelated) details you shared earlier.

Lack of Feedback

AI inherently relies on human feedback. Imagine working hard and not getting any recognition or being given a mere pat on the shoulder. You might end up not knowing if your board members, superiors, or customers are satisfied with your efforts. As a result, determining what to change, keep, or improve becomes even more arduous. Similarly, not giving AI any feedback on the work done can limit its performance. Therefore, you must tell the model what worked and what didn't; you'll see how it immediately incorporates your feedback to improve.

Being Too Loyal to a Specific LLM

Some people over-rely on a certain LLM for every task. While ChatGPT is a common choice for most people, you can't trust it all the time. Perplexity AI might be superior for deep research topics, Google Gemini for embedding SEO-ranking sources, and Grok for real-time updates. With a detailed and clear prompt, ChatGPT can still generate images, but Midjourney, DALL·E, or Higgsfield might be superior for artistic requests.

Experiment with different tools, and research which ones perform certain tasks better. Unlike people, who might take it personally when you mistrust them for certain tasks, AI models aren't bothered if you choose one over the other. It's also worth mentioning that each model can have multiple versions with varying applications and performance quality. For instance, consider using paid deep thinking mode for complex tasks versus the free, fast, and instant versions for simpler ones.

Over-Reliance

Some people ignore AI's capabilities and limitations and end up having unrealistic expectations. At the end of the day, AI is just a tool that needs responsible users. Perhaps AI isn't the perfect answer to your current query. Your task may be too sensitive, specific, or delicate, requiring another human's perspective. Sometimes, a traditional search engine carries your answer.

Certain queries, like "Your Money or Your Life" (YMYL) topics, require authoritative and reliable sources. The important thing is knowing when to reach out to alternative information sources instead of heavily relying on AI. It won't hurt to do traditional brainstorming with your team, get real client feedback, or consult your legal, financial, or medical expert for sensitive matters.

Key Takeaways

- AI is built on three core pillars: data, models, and algorithms, with machine learning and deep learning powering most modern applications, including generative AI, which creates new content from patterns learned during training.
- Effective prompting is the single most important skill for getting executive-grade results from AI, core design principles include

clarity, specificity, context, brevity, relevance, and iterative refinement.

- There are multiple prompt types: instructional, question-based, role-based, creative, analytical, conversational, contextual, and step-by-step—each suited to different tasks and objectives.
- The prompt life cycle (planning, creation, testing, evaluation, refinement, and deployment) provides a structured framework for consistently producing high-quality prompts that deliver reliable results.
- Avoid common pitfalls such as vagueness, overloading prompts with multiple queries, neglecting feedback, over-relying on a single LLM, and having unrealistic expectations of AI capabilities.

CHAPTER

2

THINKING LIKE A MACHINE

A mindset shift is what separates mediocre AI users from prompt heroes. Numerous people approach AI models the way they use Google or other search engines: They ask a question or define a task, skim through the results, accept whatever comes back as a common narrative, regardless of the quality, and move on. But high-performing leaders treat AI the way exceptional engineers treat prototypes—as something to refine, evolve, pressure-test, and optimize. Unlike search engines, AI models are designed for a back-and-forth collaboration where they can enhance the initial prompts from basic to premium through feedback.

Part of this mindset is anticipating potential knowledge gaps that AI might have. LLMs can hallucinate, misinterpret edge cases, or default to oversimplification. Having domain expertise or asking AI to embody certain roles can help you identify errors, learn by doing, and amplify the model's responses. This iterative mindset is both practical and scientifically aligned with how LLMs operate. It's also an essential mindset that you can incorporate to dominate in your field through effective prompting.

Adopting an Iterative Experimentation Approach

McKinsey's *State of AI in* 2025 report reveals that organizations that adopt rapid experimentation cycles with AI see higher productivity gains than those using it passively (Kaput, 2025). Thinking like a machine means adopting this AI mindset and experimenting with different prompt versions and patterns to enhance output quality. Rather than expecting the initial prompt to always hit the mark, incorporating feedback loops and iterating is the preferred approach to end up with effective prompts that drive desired, lasting results. The more you test and refine your prompts, the more powerful any AI model will become in your hands. This means you can harness the power of AI in your field and improve its integration by treating your initial prompts as prototypes and refining them as needed.

Start With a Basic Prompt

Most professionals aim to perfect their prompt on the first go, thinking that it will save them time. However, without iterative experimentation, they risk getting suboptimal results. A better approach is to begin with a basic prompt and assess the response quality. Start with an explicit instruction commanding AI to perform a task without adding any constraints or detailed context. As long as your prompt is focused on the task at hand, it provides a benchmark that will demonstrate the effectiveness of the different versions that follow.

Evaluate the Results

Assess the output based on different quality criteria, such as accuracy, relevance, helpfulness, completeness, and instruction-following. It's possible for a response to have one or more criteria correct and still get other elements wrong. It can be accurate and still be incomplete. Therefore, you need to judge the response closely for each qualifying criterion. Check how the model understood the explicit and implicit intents of the prompt. How well does the result meet the goal? Does the answer feel shallow? Is the structure right but missing some depth? Is the tone off? Once you see what the model interpreted, you learn what it misunderstood, what it ignored, and what it prioritized.

For instance, if you prompted a model to give the ten latest social media trends, and it yielded six recent ones and four irrelevant or outdated ones, you'd then reframe your prompt and point out why the result was incomplete or inaccurate. A thorough assessment will give you a clue on how to tweak and improve the prompt for the desired output.

Tweak Based on Output

After evaluating the results from your first prompt, the next step is to refine and tweak it, focusing on where it misses the mark. Some of the key refinement steps include adding constraints, such as specifying the tone, audience, word count, or format. For example, ask the model to generate output "in ten bullet points" or "using behavioral economics principles." Sometimes, when you realize that the initial output omits important information, tweaking a prompt means adding context that the model was unaware of.

According to research, the fastest improvements often come from changing tone or format. MIT's analysis of LLM interaction patterns found that shifting formats can significantly increase clarity and reduce reasoning errors (Zewe, 2025). A prompt written in executive language or industry jargon yields different insights than one written in a simple conversational tone. For instance, if you're using social media to promote a product and have prompted AI to create appropriate captions, you might find that an engaging and empathetic tone resonates well with your laid-back TikTok followers, whereas an authoritative, niche-based one earns you thought leadership on LinkedIn.

Leverage Trial and Error

In some traditional corporate environments, reiteration might be considered an unnecessary and costly effort that must be avoided. However, that shouldn't be the case when experimenting with AI. In essence, trial and error is more of an acceleration than a waste of resources because, eventually, you'll be scaling a tested and approved version bound to yield quality results. Each revised prompt increases precision, reduces ambiguity, and brings the model closer to your mental capacity or desired level of expertise. Trial and error helps you track the model's performance as you observe which prompts generate the best output and which ones perform suboptimally.

Experiment With Different Prompt Styles, Tones, and Formats

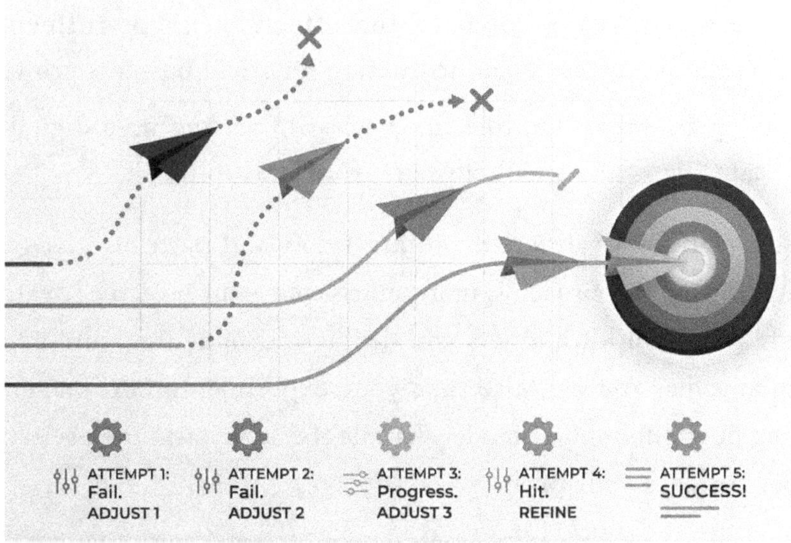

Consider a top consultant who doesn't use a cookie-cutter approach with every client but adjusts their communication style to tailor the experience each time. AI can also respond differently depending on the framing of each query. Asking a model a direct question produces one type of response; assigning it a role produces another; giving it a constraint-heavy task yields a third. Take a look at the following prompt examples from a digital marketer's experiment:

- **Direct:** "What are the current trends in digital marketing for small businesses?"
- **Role-based:** "As a digital marketing consultant, recommend the top three strategies a small business should use in 2026."
- **Constraint-heavy:** "Create a digital marketing plan for a small business with a budget under $5,000 that targets millennials on social media."
- **Instructional:** "Explain how small businesses can improve their social media engagement in five steps."
- **Creative:** "Imagine you're launching a small eco-friendly brand. How would you attract customers using digital marketing?"
- **Comparative:** "Compare the effectiveness of influencer marketing versus email marketing for small business growth."
- **Step-by-step:** "Outline the process of setting up a digital ad campaign for a small business from start to finish."

Experimenting with different prompt types and patterns gives you insight into which approach is more suitable for your objectives. Variety expands your tool kit and lets you deploy the right structure at any particular time. You can also take your experimentation further by checking how different AI models handle the same task, then selecting one that enriches your prompt.

Leverage Feedback Loops

Just like in any professional setting, feedback plays an important role in improving AI's performance and efficiency. Giving the model feedback, such as pointing out a lack of depth, can encourage it to yield an insightful response. For example, "This sounds bland and not authoritative enough; can you enrich it with a relatable example and add a reputable statistic to back it up?" If the prompt produces a technical response, you can ask the model to demystify it and write in a language digestible for a general (or specific) audience. By asking the model to clarify, deepen, contrast, critique, simulate, or quantify, you push the system to refine its reasoning and reveal higher-quality insights.

Track and Document Changes

You might notice that certain phrases, structures, or role assignments consistently produce more reliable results. You might also learn that your best outputs occur when you include specific constraints or specify particular formats. While tracking changes can be tedious as you experiment with multiple prompts, documenting prompt types or patterns that consistently yield quality results can be helpful. Therefore, create your mini playbook by noting the changes and highlighting important information that you can pull out and implement later—without going through the lengthy testing processes again.

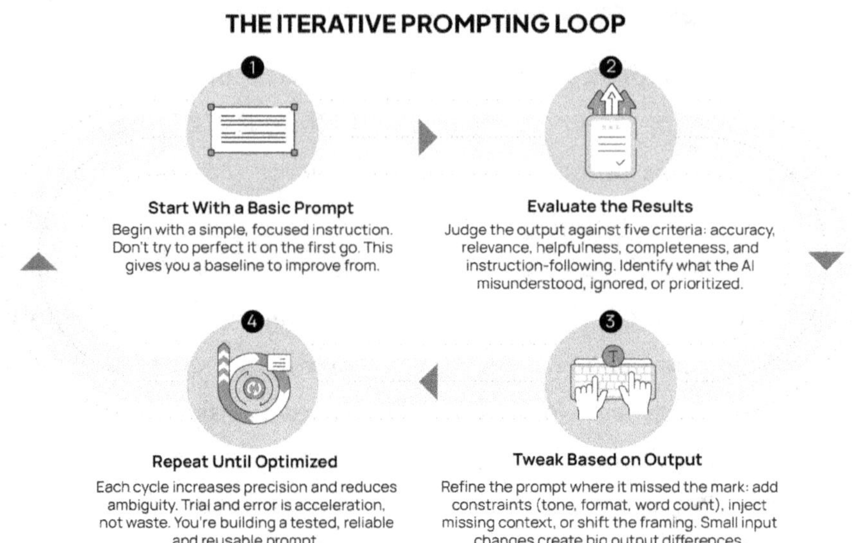

Embrace Domain Expertise

Research reveals that LLMs perform significantly better and more accurately when the user demonstrates domain awareness in the prompt (Singh, 2025). If you don't consider the specific domain when querying AI, you won't know how to frame your prompts or how to judge the quality of the model's response. Using terminology and jargon specific to your field recalibrates how the model interprets your question.

When you mention earnings before interest, taxes, depreciation, and amortization (EBITDA) margins, customer acquisition cost and lifetime value (CAC:LTV) ratios, or generally accepted accounting principles (GAAP) revenue recognition, the model retrieves patterns associated with finance rather than generic content. When you reference diffusion models, embeddings, token windows, or inference latency, the model shifts into technical mode. Furthermore, when you speak in regulatory language—the General Data Protection Regulation (GDPR), Payment Card Industry Data Security Standard (PCI DSS), or Health Insurance Portability and Accountability Act (HIPAA)—the model elevates compliance sensitivity. Embracing domain expertise when prompting AI enriches the outcome by ensuring that its context remains industry-related.

Understand the Subject Area

If someone asks you a random question without a specific niche or context, you're likely to return a safe and generic answer. However, if you truly have a rich background in a certain field, such as financial strategy, product design, business operations, data analytics, cybersecurity, or supply chain, your response will be more insightful and authoritative.

Similarly, AI models produce output based on the subject area or industry jargon level embedded in the prompt. The more you understand your domain, the more specific and high-impact your prompts become. Therefore, you must be willing to communicate skillfully with AI to portray your knowledge. Even if you don't have the necessary qualifications, be sure to research or thoroughly learn about the topic you'll be giving AI tasks on so you can use the executive language for richer output.

Anticipate Potential Knowledge Gaps

AI doesn't know your proprietary data, internal workflows, or organizational nuance unless you explicitly embed it into prompts. You must anticipate what the model might misunderstand and proactively correct or supplement those gaps in your prompt. For instance, ensure that you spell out industry constraints, emerging regulations, market dynamics, and business model peculiarities that you want the model to consider.

Having domain expertise and anticipating potential knowledge gaps enables you to be thorough when prompting AI models; it also ensures that your prompts are ethically sound. For example, when commanding a model to draft an overview of compliance requirements for a new consumer data privacy law, you might want to specify that you mean the one enacted in 2023 that impacts your marketing practices, including requirements for explicit consent, data retention limits, and penalties for non-compliance (Newmark, 2025).

Pre-empt this by specifying constraints such as "Use data from after 2023 only," "Exclude hypothetical scenarios," and "Base your reasoning on fundamental accounting principles." This reduces error because it narrows the model's interpretive space.

Detailed niche-specific knowledge restricts you from accepting incorrect output and prepares you to acknowledge that the model might not be privy to the latest updates regarding regulations. You have to be aware of the possibility of the model yielding outdated information that could potentially be harmful. Anticipating the model's blind spots enables you to create prompts that produce more reliable output with fewer iterations.

Encourage AI to Embrace a Specific Expertise Level

As discussed in the previous chapter, role assignment dramatically elevates the intelligence of AI outputs because it forces the model to activate relevant patterns. When you instruct it to "Act as a senior compliance officer," "Act as a Fortune 500 CFO," or "Act as a McKinsey-style strategy consultant," you give it a clear interpretive lens. The model automatically retrieves reasoning patterns matching that persona, which improves depth and tone. Role-based prompting is one of the most effective ways to align the AI's perspective with the expertise level required for complex or high-stakes work.

If you want to get more technical, you can infuse your specific industry jargon into the prompt. Think of healthcare, legal, finance, crypto, or marketing sectors and embed certain terms that would guide the model to enhance output tone and authority. For example, "Write a pricing strategy for our online course" becomes "Recommend a pricing model based on LTV vs. CAC and whether demand elasticity varies across core ideal client profile (ICP) segments." When instructed with a specific expertise level, the model refrains from giving general or safe outputs and embodies authority to yield the expected high-quality output.

Understand How Prompt Patterns Affect Output

Thinking like a machine necessitates understanding how AI models digest data and generate responses based on input prompts. This insight enables you to frame your instructions in such a way that the model performs at its best potential. It underscores the criticality of framing prompts thoughtfully to enhance the accuracy, creativity, and utility of AI-generated content. You can also collaborate with AI and ask it to help you reframe your prompts for useful output. From exploratory to problem-solving prompt patterns, understanding how AI interprets commands can help you create prompts that produce high-quality output.

Explorative Pattern

Because LLMs can process billions of datasets, it's easier to get multiple viewpoints and explore various possibilities without limits. The explorative prompt pattern encourages you to give the model an open-ended query without any predefined boundaries. It allows you to harness AI's ability to dive deeper into any topic to bring discovery and innovation. This is ideal when you want groundbreaking ideas that will take your business or strategies to greater heights.

For example, if you're exploring the potential markets for a new sustainable product, you can ask AI an exploratory question like "What are the emerging trends in eco-friendly consumer goods?" or "How could we create value in unexpected ways with this product?" The output would reflect that the model explored a plethora of possibilities without confining itself to any local or preset parameters. This approach allows you to learn innovative things you wouldn't have discovered through regular research based on what you already know.

Comparative Pattern

The comparative pattern involves prompts that ask for similarities and differences among two or more items, concepts, or strategies. Using AI in this manner enables you to evaluate options, advantages, and drawbacks more clearly. You can use the comparative prompt pattern when deciding between competing business models or marketing strategies. For instance, let's say you're a start-up founder seeking direction on whether to use an in-house development team or outsource talent. You can ask, "Can you compare the benefits and downsides of using an in-house development team versus outsourcing for a start-up?" The output will give you clarity on the best path forward as it will include the pros and cons of each option, such as cost, speed, and quality.

Instructional Pattern

The instructional pattern is designed to provide clear, step-by-step guidance. It involves directing the AI model to produce actionable, procedural outputs. As an entrepreneur or leader, the success of your organization hinges on the ability to give and follow instructions, from launching a product to managing operations or scaling a business. When designed well, instructional prompts shorten the discovery-to-execution cycle, meaning that what once required workshops and meetings becomes a structured playbook in minutes. Therefore, leveraging instructional prompts can bring significant results and improve efficiency. For example, an instructional prompt like "List the key steps for training new hires effectively in a retail environment" can benefit a small business owner creating a manual for onboarding new employees.

Moreover, the instructional prompt pattern requires you to specify the desired format (checklist, timeline, decision tree, etc.), acceptance criteria, and any organizational constraints. When creating a new employee onboarding checklist with the prompt above, it's imperative to specify the format as a step-by-step checklist, set acceptance criteria such as completion of all tasks before the end of the first week, and include constraints like compliance with the company's security policies and equipment availability. This ensures the model produces a practical, ready-to-use onboarding guide relevant to your professional environment.

Problem-Solving Pattern

Focused on identifying, analyzing, and resolving specific issues, the problem-solving pattern is critical when facing challenges. It encourages quick diagnostic thinking and strategizing solutions without dwelling too much on analyzing the problem manually. Regardless of the problematic tasks at hand, you can take advantage of AI's superpower and create solutions instantly. The model's output is most valuable when it includes trade-offs, resource estimates, and suggested KPIs for measuring success, allowing you to make pragmatic choices quickly. Applied at the right stage, this pattern shifts AI from diagnosis to execution support, which essentially turns insight into a measurable outcome.

Take a look at this detailed problem-solving prompt: "Context: Our city's public transportation system is experiencing increasing delays and declining rider satisfaction, as shown by a 15% drop in on-time arrivals over the past year and a 20% decrease in survey ratings. Budget constraints limit available upgrades to $5 million annually. Task: Recommend a prioritized set of actionable interventions to improve on-time performance and rider satisfaction. Include implementation steps, potential pitfalls, trade-offs between different solutions, estimated costs and resources required, and KPIs that city leaders can use to measure success over the next two years."

It would yield a rich, solution-oriented output that considers all relevant aspects, unlike a less effective prompt like "What are the possible causes of reduced user retention, and how can we address them through design or marketing changes?"

Collaborative Pattern

What if you don't know how to ask the right question or frame your prompts for the model to help you effectively? This is where you acknowledge the possibility of AI outsmarting you, albeit only on that specific task. This enables you to collaborate with an AI model and ask it to guide you through a task. If you want to improve your prompt but don't know where to start, you can use AI to help audit the initial prompt for quality and identify any missing instructions it could use to serve you better.

You can start with a simple request, like "Write a cold email." Then ask the model, "If you were me, what additional information would you need?" Supply that information and rerun the prompt. You just unlocked collaborative prompting. This pattern teaches you to use AI to assign the best perspective for it. Let's say you want to answer a question as an authoritative persona, but you aren't sure which expertise role to use. You can command AI: "Before answering, tell me which role should be answering this question," and then use that role. For example, if AI says, "You need a CFO perspective," you can reply, "Answer as a CFO."

You can also use collaborative prompts to anticipate customer feedback and improve your product before launching it. This way, you address potential objections beforehand and launch an irresistible product that hits the right spot.

Creative Pattern

Creative prompts are intentionally open enough to elicit novel combinations yet structured so that the ideas produced remain relevant to business objectives. The trick is to specify boundaries, such as the audience archetype, brand voice, budget, or regulatory guardrails, so that the model's creativity perfectly aligns. This means guiding the model to consider feasible, actionable concepts rather than unfettered imagination that yields wildly overstated outputs.

For example, a start-up founder looking to create a memorable advertising campaign might use creative prompts such as "Generate unique storytelling ideas that combine humor and emotional appeal to attract young adults." This guides the model to think innovatively while appealing to the specified audience, merging creativity with relevance.

For best results, you can incorporate other prompt variations, such as personas, constraints-heavy, explorative, or problem-solving, depending on your specific needs. "Imagine you're a guru copywriter for a cybersecurity start-up; create engaging and highly converting 300-word email marketing copy that merges Alex Cattoni's humor style and Gen Z slang to appeal to the younger audience." Well-designed creative prompt patterns like this can accelerate innovative organizational initiatives without the up-front ideation overhead.

PROMPT PATTERNS AT A GLANCE

PATTERN	BEST FOR	OUTPUT STYLE	WHEN TO USE
Explorative	Discovery, innovation, broad research	Wide-ranging, multi-perspective, open-ended	When you want groundbreaking ideas without predefined boundaries
Comparative	Evaluating options, pros/cons, trade-offs	Structured side-by-side analysis	When deciding between competing strategies, tools, or models
Instructional	Step-by-step guidance, SOPs, playbooks	Sequential, actionable, procedural	When you need clear how-to output with defined steps
Problem-Solving	Diagnosing issues, strategizing solutions	Diagnostic, solution-oriented with trade-offs and KPIs	When facing a specific challenge that needs analysis and resolution
Collaborative	Getting AI to guide you, co-creating prompts	Interactive, question-driven, advisory	When you don't know how to frame the right question or need AI's input on the prompt itself
Creative	Ideation, branding, campaigns, storytelling	Imaginative but bounded by audience and brand constraints	When you need novel ideas that remain relevant to business objectives

Practical Exercises

The following exercises will help reinforce the iterative process of prompt engineering, highlight the value of domain expertise, and illustrate how prompt patterns affect AI-generated content. Use the provided examples as guidance to generate your own relevant prompts.

Exercise 1: Iterative Prompt Improvement

Objective

To practice adopting an iterative experimentation approach in prompt design, using domain expertise, and understanding the impact of different prompt patterns on the output quality.

Instructions

1. Pick a simple business task, such as writing an email, summarizing research, generating product ideas, or drafting a social media caption.
2. Write an initial prompt without overthinking it, and run it through your AI tool.
3. Evaluate the output using five criteria: clarity, accuracy, relevance, specificity, and tone.
4. Now, rewrite the prompt with improvements, and rerun it.
5. Modify the prompt using different prompt patterns to observe how the output changes.
6. Incorporate domain-specific terminology and expertise in each iteration to refine the prompt further. Replace a general prompt ("Write a marketing strategy") with a domain-specific one ("As a growth marketer for a SaaS productivity start-up, build a three-month acquisition strategy focused on product-led growth, content funnels, and onboarding activation").
7. Repeat steps 4–6 at least three times, comparing outputs each time.

Reflective Questions

- Does the tone change?
- Does the level of authority change?
- Does the depth increase?

As you compare outputs, you'll see which prompts are more useful and strategic, and which feel like they were written for your business rather than for a random person online.

Exercise 2: Prompt Pattern Testing

Objective

To observe how different prompt patterns change outcome quality.

Instructions

Choose one topic, such as "Online business ideas." Now ask about the same topic using multiple patterns:

- **Exploratory pattern:** "Explain the evolution of online business models since 2000."
- **Comparative pattern:** "Compare affiliate marketing and print-on-demand for beginners."
- **Instructional pattern:** "Give me step-by-step instructions to start an online business."
- **Problem-solving pattern:** "Some countries are still suffering from the post-pandemic economic crisis, with unemployment rates as high as 49% in low-income African countries. There are wide gaps in the global workforce, primarily affecting youth and women. Given this context, suggest five profitable, disaster-proof, and zero-capital online businesses that can solve this problem and outline how long it would take."

- **Creative pattern:** "Invent 10 business ideas using AI automation."
- **Collaborative pattern:** "If you were a difficult customer, what kind of complaints would you have about a product sold by an online business?" "Help me anticipate possible customer objections regarding this product and marketplace and suggest ways to handle them."
- **Role-based pattern:** "Act as a business accelerator mentor evaluating my idea."

Reflective Question

Which pattern produced the most useful business outcome for you?

You can also do micro-testing: Pick a prompt and change only one word to see the outcome. For instance, change "outline" to "detailed plan," "ideas" to "strategic recommendations," and "write" to "critique," and observe the difference. In most cases, small input distinctions create massive output variations.

Key Takeaways

- Adopt an iterative experimentation mindset: start with a basic prompt, evaluate the output against quality criteria (accuracy, relevance, completeness), and refine through multiple cycles rather than trying to perfect prompts on the first attempt.
- Domain expertise dramatically improves AI output quality; embedding industry-specific terminology, anticipating knowledge gaps, and assigning expert roles forces the model to activate more relevant and authoritative response patterns.
- Different prompt patterns—explorative, comparative, instructional, problem-solving, collaborative, and creative—each

produce distinct output characteristics, and selecting the right pattern for your objective is critical to getting the best results.

- Feedback loops and tracking your prompt iterations help you build a personal library of high-performing prompts and develop an intuition for what works across different AI tools and use cases.
- Experimenting with different prompt styles, tones, formats, and even different LLMs expands your prompting toolkit and helps you discover which approach delivers the best results for each specific task.

CHAPTER

3

BECOME A PROMPT HERO WITH THESE ADVANCED TECHNIQUES

The AI market is growing exponentially, with over 4,800 generative AI tools launched in the first half of 2025 (Thakur, 2025). Given this influx, keeping up with the industry can be overwhelming. However, becoming a prompting hero is no longer about mastering specific AI tools or platforms. It's about crafting evergreen prompts that work with any system.

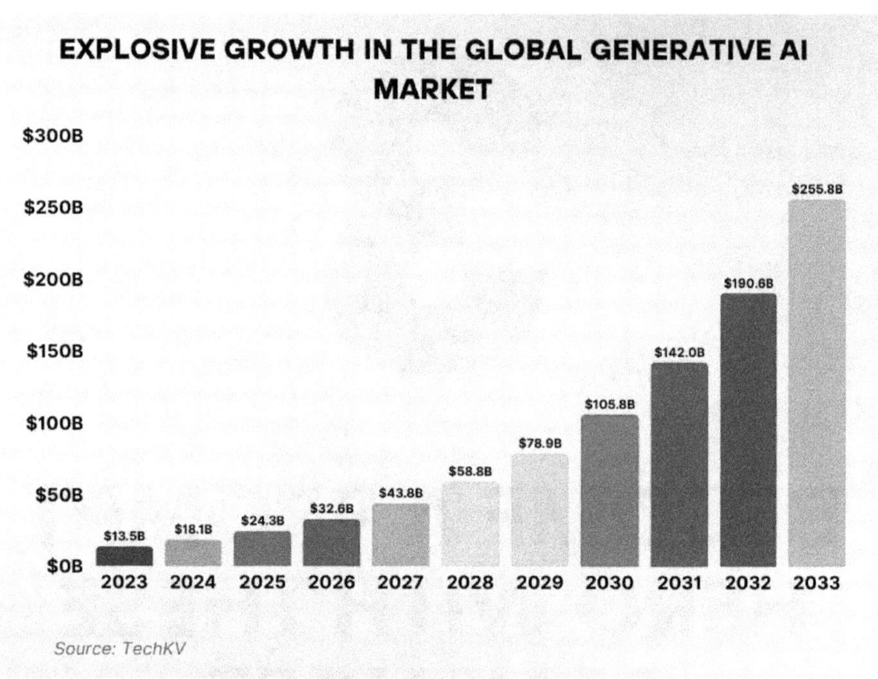

Technically, computer systems are programmed through commands and rules, which enable them to carry out tasks in an expected manner. Although NLP and machine learning now enable us to communicate with systems without hard-coding, prompting is still a way to program AI models to do what we ask in a manner we expect (or dictate). The difference is that the text-based rules are understood even by non-coders, empowering you to dictate any role for the system to embody and provide context, format, examples, and constraints.

Once you master the advanced techniques, do practical exercises, and learn from the various examples in this chapter, it won't matter if 1,000 AI tools emerge daily. You'll be able to command current and future models and get phenomenal results from any tool you use. These advanced prompting techniques will empower you to transform vague, one-size-fits-all queries into precision tools that unlock value, innovate processes, and build meaningful connections.

Prompt Engineering Methods

Depending on the scenario, task, or level of depth required, there are several prompt engineering methods to choose from. From simple prompts for generalized tasks to multistep and hybrid prompts, each serves a different purpose, making it essential to know when to use each one effectively. You can use them either in isolation or collaboratively, depending on your project needs and desired outcomes.

Zero-Shot Prompting

Zero-shot prompting means commanding an AI model to perform a task without providing any examples. In this case, you base the output on the model's training data and its ability to perform common and non-complex tasks. This approach relies on the model's generalized knowledge and its ability to follow specified instructions, even if it isn't shown how to carry out a task. Zero-shot prompting is ideal when you want quick answers or are assessing a model's explorative capabilities.

Consider the initial basic prompts discussed in the previous chapter, which included clear instructions but no examples. You can ask the model, "List all the states that make up the United States of America," and it will list them in no particular order. But if you want the list to be alphabetical or to follow any special format that requires an example, then the prompt won't be regarded as zero-shot anymore. A prompt like "Define compounding interest" is easier than "Calculate compounding interest," because the calculation would require the equation format to be specified. Therefore, if you presume the task to be complex but don't have any examples, you can still use zero-shot prompting to obtain the initial output and iterate as needed; alternatively, you can use the output as the example for one-shot prompting or other techniques.

If you ever consider building your own model, this technique can come in handy, because models can be trained without any specific examples through zero-shot learning. This would enable rapid deployment of AI tools without the need for exhaustive data preparation. For example, an entrepreneur launching a new ecommerce platform might use zero-shot prompting for their customer support AI, enabling it to handle unprecedented queries without prior training on specific FAQs.

One-Shot Prompting

One-shot prompting means asking an AI model to perform a task and accompanying your query with one example to emulate in the output. You would typically use one-shot prompting when you want the model to follow a particular pattern or generate the output in a unique format. For example, let's say you want to list the states of the USA in alphabetical order; you'd typically include Alabama as the first state and ask the model to continue. If you wanted the format to be the state name and abbreviation, you'd say, "Write the state names together with their abbreviations, e.g., Alabama (AL)..." and the model would list the remaining states and abbreviations accordingly.

Another example of one-shot prompting is: "Translate the following:

- Spanish: *Hola*→English: Hi

- Spanish: *Dinero*→English:"

The model will complete the remaining unsolved task and translate "dinero" to "money" following the format example provided.

From the developer's perspective, for those desiring to build their own models, one-shot prompting allows AI systems to understand and generalize from a single example. This method is more common and effective in scenarios where data is scarce or unique. Executives investing in cutting-edge personalized marketing tools can appreciate one-shot prompting's ability to quickly adapt to individual customer behaviors with minimal data. For instance, a start-up in luxury fashion could employ one-shot prompting to tailor recommendations for exclusive, one-off product lines after being exposed to just one customer interaction.

Few-Shot Prompting

Few-shot prompting is an expansion of one-shot prompting that adds a small number of examples to the prompt so that the model truly captures your intent and follows a specific format. Expanding the previous example of the U.S. states, you'd include "Alabama (AL), Alaska (AK), Arizona (AZ)..."; the model would then ensure that it didn't deviate from that alphabetical order and would accurately add abbreviations. With the translation exercise, you'd also provide more examples for the model to follow.

- "Spanish: *Hola*→English: Hi
- Spanish: *Dinero*→English: Money
- Spanish: *Venta*→English: Sale
- Spanish: *Tarjeta de crédito*→English:
- Spanish: *Margen de beneficio*→English:"

The model would translate the remaining phrases, "credit card" and "profit margin," using the same format.

Few-shot prompting is critical where tasks require nuance and structure. It strikes a balance between data efficiency and model accuracy. Entrepreneurs seeking to scale innovations rapidly can benefit from few-shot learning by reducing the time and resources needed to gather extensive datasets. For example, a SaaS company might implement few-shot learning to enhance its AI-driven analytics platform to interpret new types of client data formats soon after launch.

The same principle applies when training models, with the trainer providing several examples to solidify the lesson and ensure that the model yields an output that hits the mark. In this case, few-shot learning is usually incorporated to strike a balance between data efficiency and model accuracy.

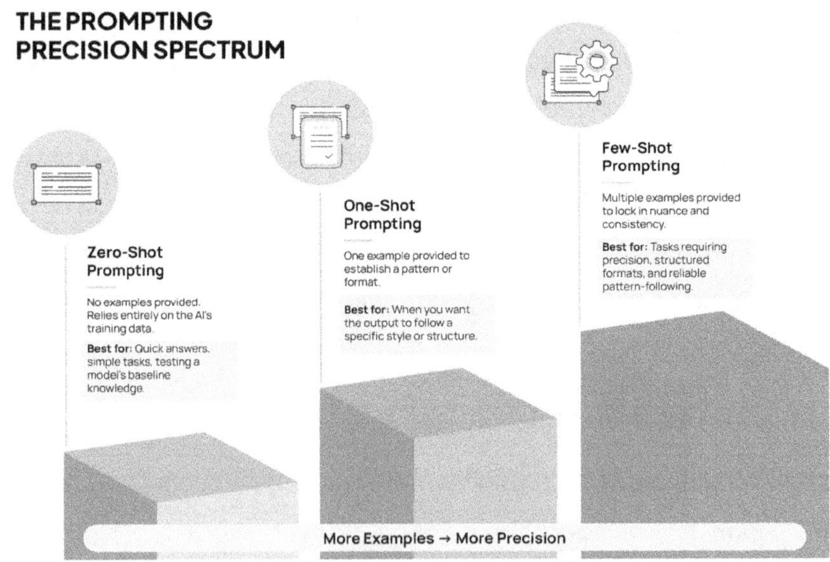

Role-Based and Persona-Driven Prompting

We've already established what role-based or persona-driven prompting is. Given a clear set of rules and a well-defined persona to embody, AI models are a marvel at getting into character and delivering exceptional results. If you ask AI to respond as you, then you need to give it enough details about who you are. Don't just prompt it to perform a task as a CEO without further context; instead, say, "As a CEO [or any specific role] of [COMPANY] specializing in [INDUSTRY], do the following [TASK], considering [CONSTRAINTS]." For example, "As a CEO of GreenTech Innovations specializing in renewable energy, develop a sustainable growth strategy for the next five years, considering budget limitations and environmental regulations."

Giving detailed prompts helps the model excel at its task, as it assumes it has insight into what happens in your organization. If you want to predict what your customers might complain about regarding an upcoming product or service, give the model enough context, including what routine product handling and delivery would be like. As the model embodies your customer, it anticipates their pain points from similar businesses and might incorporate any related online reviews to yield a content-rich result. This way, you gain insight into things you wouldn't have considered and thus can make provisions ahead of time. This has more impact in situations where you might be biased when considering different roles, like switching your perspective from owner to customer, or when working with roles in which you have limited experience.

Persona-driven prompts are powerful for stress-testing plans, anticipating objections, or crafting communications targeted to specific audiences because they force the model to surface perspective-specific priorities and counterarguments. For example, if you're a start-up founder who uses role-based prompting when seeking advice from a virtual AI assistant, you might frame prompts as if the assistant were a seasoned growth marketer. This approach would yield targeted strategies focused on user acquisition and retention, rather than generic advice.

Pro tip: You can also configure your LLM to embody a certain persona for a project you're working on. For example, if you're building a GPT or any app where you want the system to act as a companion assistant, a role-based system prompt can help you get the same quality for multiple chats related to that project.

In a team setting, role-based prompting can streamline project workflows. You might prompt an AI tool to generate a product road map from the product manager's perspective, ensuring outputs align with practical priorities and challenges on the ground. This specificity helps bridge communication gaps and accelerate execution.

Retrieval-Augmented Generation and Knowledge Grounding

Retrieval-augmented generation (RAG) and knowledge grounding are advanced prompt techniques used to enhance the quality and relevance of AI-generated content. They involve inserting external documents, datasets, or knowledge sources into the model's reasoning process so that it doesn't depend exclusively on internal training data. Instead of utilizing "what the model knows," the output uses curated information and anchors output to real data, organizational knowledge, PDFs, customer relationship management (CRM) system data, financial modeling, or any authoritative repository. RAG combines the capabilities of retrieval systems and generative models, while knowledge grounding ensures that the generated content is firmly based on specified trusted information, databases, or documents.

Using these techniques ensures that the models avoid hallucination and deliver consistent, accurate content aligned with verified sources. The framework first retrieves relevant documents or data from a knowledge base and then generates answers or content based on that retrieved information. This approach ensures the output is both informative and grounded in accurate and recent data, which is crucial for business decisions and communications.

You can use RAG to produce up-to-date market analysis and reports, generate policy drafts informed by current regulations, and create tailored responses based on a company's internal documents or FAQs. For example, "Retrieve the latest quarterly financial data and generate a comprehensive analysis highlighting trends in revenue growth and customer acquisition for our SaaS product." "Use the company's HR policy documents and draft a memo outlining the updated remote work guidelines for 2026."

Knowledge grounding can amplify your prompting game when drafting technical manuals referencing product specifications, writing marketing copy based on verified customer testimonials and case studies, and summarizing legal contracts or compliance requirements precisely. The key is to attach these information sources and prompt the model as follows: "Ground your summary in the attached annual report and create an executive summary focusing on key strategic initiatives and financial outcomes." "Based on the product specification document, generate a detailed FAQ section to assist the customer support team." Knowledge grounding is also helpful when you need to have multiple chats and require the model to remember your information.

Chain-of-Thought Prompting

Chain-of-thought (CoT) prompting is a technique that involves explicitly instructing the model to reason through a problem step-by-step before arriving at a conclusion. Rather than jumping straight to an answer, the AI is guided to surface assumptions, evaluate trade-offs, and follow a logical progression. This approach significantly improves analytical rigor, reduces shallow pattern-matching, and lowers the risk of confident but unfounded conclusions. Any decision that feels complex, high-stakes, or hard to explain is a candidate for CoT prompting.

When you ask the model to articulate its reasoning, you force it to expose the variables that come with business decision-making. For example, pricing, hiring, product strategy, and market entry aren't binary but vary per case. Thus, CoT makes conclusions easier to evaluate, challenge, and refine, with the results providing a clearer mental model you can actually use.

Consider the following prompt: "Think step-by-step. What factors should a start-up consider before increasing pricing?" A standard prompt might return a surface-level list: competition, costs, and customer demand. Contrarily, the CoT prompt is far more likely to walk through sequencing: customer segmentation, price sensitivity by cohort, perceived value versus delivered value, churn risk, competitive positioning, margin structure, and long-term brand implications.

From an entrepreneurial standpoint, this prompting method is especially valuable in areas where second-order effects matter. Pricing strategy is an obvious example. A price increase may boost short-term revenue while quietly increasing churn, reducing word-of-mouth growth, or repositioning the brand in unintended ways. CoT prompting helps surface these cascading effects before decisions are locked in.

The same applies to expansion planning. Whether you're entering a new market, adding a product line, or scaling operations, the ability to reason through dependencies such as regulatory complexity, operational capacity, cultural fit, capital requirements, can prevent costly missteps. Asking the model to reason step-by-step mirrors the internal decision memos used by high-performing executive teams. CoT prompting is the closest you'll get to consultant-grade thinking on demand. When used consistently, it trains you to think more clearly as well. Over time, you begin to anticipate the steps, constraints, and questions that matter long before the AI responds.

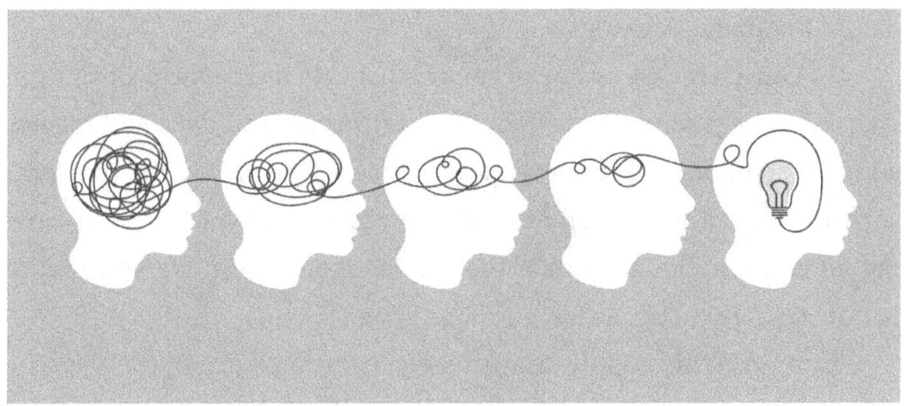

Program-of-Thought Prompting

The program-of-thought (PoT) prompting technique is an advanced method designed to enhance an AI model's reasoning and problem-solving capabilities. It involves instructing the model to simulate writing a small program or a sequence of logical steps to tackle a business problem, much like how a business analyst or strategist would approach complex problems. Similar to CoT, PoT guides the model to provide answers as well as to outline a step-by-step programmatic thought process, instead of merely giving a direct answer. Research reveals that PoT outperforms CoT by up to 15% (Cleary, 2025).

The model explains its reasoning in a structured manner that resembles algorithmic thinking or workflow processes. This method is particularly beneficial in domains where decision-making, process optimization, and scenario analysis are crucial. It enhances clarity by breaking down complex business challenges into manageable, logical steps. It also improves transparency, enabling stakeholders to understand the reasoning behind AI-generated recommendations. Furthermore, it facilitates the automation of decision-support processes by translating thought processes into executable logic. You can also use PoT to mitigate risks using a stepwise evaluation, which identifies potential pitfalls before finalizing decisions.

To construct PoT prompts, you must clearly define the problem you want AI to help solve. Include all relevant context and data, and request a logical solution. You can even ask the model to outline the problem-solving process as a program or algorithm. You must also specify any output expectations or format the answer should take. Do you want a list of steps, pseudocode, or a decision tree?

Consider this supply-chain-centered prompt example: "Given a dataset of supplier costs, delivery times, and reliability scores, write a step-by-step program to select the optimal supplier mix that minimizes cost while maintaining delivery reliability above 95%. Explain the reasoning at each step." This is how a financial risk assessment prompt would look: "Create a logical program to evaluate the credit risk of a loan applicant based on income, debt-to-income ratio, credit score, and employment status. Include decision rules and conditions used to classify applicants into risk categories."

Here's another PoT prompt example: "Devise a stepwise algorithm to segment customers based on purchase history, demographics, and engagement metrics to identify the top 10% most likely to respond to a new product launch. Explain how each variable influences the segmentation."

As you can see in all these examples, there are trigger phrases, such as "step-by-step program," "logical program," and "stepwise algorithm," that amplify CoT prompts into PoT prompts.

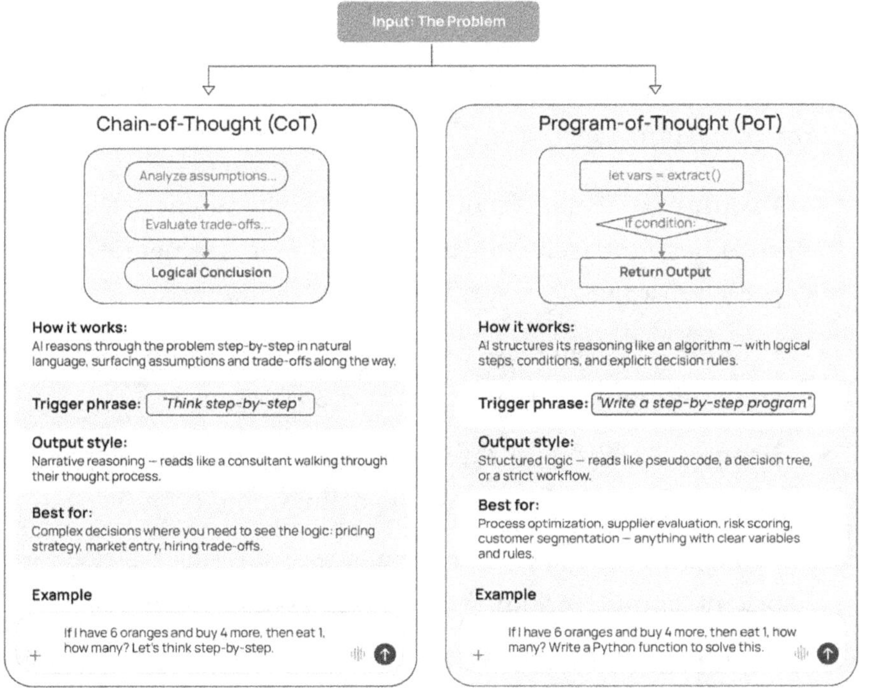

Chaining Prompts for Multistep Reasoning

Prompt chaining is a deliberate technique of breaking a complex problem into a sequence of smaller prompts, where the output of one prompt becomes the structured input for the next. Unlike CoT and PoT, which ask the model to reason step-by-step within a single response, prompt chaining distributes reasoning across multiple interactions. While CoT and PoT improve depth of reasoning, prompt chaining improves control, reliability, and scalability.

You can use prompt chaining when the task itself has distinct phases that require different lenses, constraints, or evaluation criteria, unlike asking the model to do everything at once. Let's consider the CoT prompt example: "Think step-by-step. What factors should a SaaS start-up consider before increasing prices?" We established that the output will be thoughtful and structured, but it remains a single synthesis (one answer, one frame, and one interpretation).

Now, observe how different it looks as a multistep process using the prompt chaining approach:

- **Prompt 1:** "Analyze our current pricing model. Identify weaknesses based on churn, customer segmentation, and perceived value."
- **Prompt 2:** "Given these weaknesses, analyze competitor pricing and positioning in the mid-market SaaS segment."
- **Prompt 3:** "Propose three alternative pricing strategies that address these weaknesses while maintaining growth."
- **Prompt 4:** "Evaluate the risks and second-order effects of each pricing option, including churn and brand perception."
- **Prompt 5:** "Based on the analysis above, recommend a pricing strategy and explain why it dominates the alternatives."

Each step narrows uncertainty, applies different constraints, and reduces potential for hallucination. More importantly, each output can be reviewed, edited, or replaced before moving forward. In expansion planning, for example, you might chain prompts to identify attractive markets, filter by regulatory complexity, assess operational readiness, model financial outcomes, and produce a go/no-go recommendation.

In product development, prompt chains can translate customer feedback into themes, rank themes by impact and feasibility, generate feature concepts, write product requirement documents (PRDs), and draft internal launch plans. In marketing, prompt chaining allows teams to separate ideation from optimization. One prompt generates raw ideas, while another tests messaging against ICP pain points; a third refines tone, and a fourth produces channel-specific assets. Eventually, the result is content that aligns strategically across the funnel.

One of the hidden key benefits of chaining prompts is error isolation. When everything's done in one prompt, errors compound invisibly, whereas when prompts are chained, mistakes become obvious at the step where they occur. This enables you to intervene, adjust assumptions, or inject new data at any stage without restarting the entire process. This is one of the reasons this technique is valuable in high-stakes environments such as finance, compliance, and strategic planning.

Schema-First Design

Schema-first prompting involves defining a structured outline or framework before deep AI interaction. Think of categorizing input data and content, such as market analysis, product specs, and customer segments, up-front to guide generation. For instance, if you're drafting a business plan, you might use a schema dividing sections into "Problem Statement," "Competitive Landscape," and "Revenue Model," ensuring coherent and comprehensive output. This design mirrors database normalization and facilitates easier iteration by enforcing a clear architecture. It helps entrepreneurs maintain strategic focus while leveraging AI's generative power efficiently.

LLMs don't always reason top-down like humans. They generate text probabilistically, token by token, based on patterns learned from training data. When the model is left to decide both what to say and how to structure it, the cognitive load is high, and results vary widely. Schema-first prompting reduces that uncertainty by narrowing the output space, anchoring the model to a predefined format, reducing ambiguity around expectations, and preventing verbosity and hallucination.

Google DeepMind researchers have noted that structured prompting improves task reliability because the model optimizes generation within known boundaries rather than improvising structure as it goes (Yang et al., 2023). From a business standpoint, this indicates that AI systems perform best when embedded into clearly defined workflows, not when treated as free-form assistants.

Many professionals think they're writing good prompts because they provide context and detail. Schema-first prompting takes it a step further by separating thinking from formatting. Instead of "Analyze this market and give me recommendations," you specify sections, ordering, required fields, decision criteria, and constraints (including length, tone, and metrics). In other words, where regular prompting asks what the AI thinks, schema-first prompting controls how that thinking is expressed. Consider the following prompt schema:

Section 1 (Context):

- Briefly describe the market scenario (max. three sentences).

Section 2 (Analysis Requirements):

- Identify key market trends (list at least three).
- Highlight major challenges (list at least two).

Section 3 (Recommendations):

- Provide at least three actionable recommendations.
- Each recommendation must include a brief description (max. two sentences), expected impact (use measurable metrics if possible), and implementation constraints (time, cost, resources).

Section 4 (Tone and Length):

- Tone must be professional and concise.
- The total response length must be 300 words max.

Let's use a practical scenario: A founder is evaluating whether to enter a new regional market and wants a decision-ready analysis, not a brainstorm. Here's a typical (poor) prompt:

"Analyze whether we should expand into South America."

From what we've covered thus far, you can already see how this invites vagueness, uneven depth, and missing data. Now, observe the difference in the schema-first prompt design:

"You're a senior strategy consultant advising a growth-stage B2B SaaS company. Analyze market expansion into South America using the following schema.

Output strictly in this format:

One (Market Attractiveness):

- Estimate the total addressable/available market (TAM)
- Growth rate
- Key demand drivers

Two (Competitive Landscape):

- Top five competitors
- Differentiation gaps
- Pricing benchmarks

Three (Operational Complexity):

- Regulatory risks
- Localization requirements
- Talent and infrastructure considerations

Four (Financial Impact):

- Estimated 12-month revenue potential
- Cost drivers
- Break-even assumptions

Five (Risks and Mitigations):

- Top three risks
- Mitigation strategies

Six (Recommendation):

- Go / No-Go

Seven (Rationale):

- Write a rationale in no more than 150 words."

Do you notice what this does? It forces completeness, prevents overemphasis on one dimension, produces an output that could go directly into a board deck, and enables easy comparison with future market analyses. Simply put, this schema controls the AI's outputs from structure to detail and style, exemplifying schema-first prompting. It's no surprise that schema-first prompting excels in environments where outputs must be reviewed by stakeholders, consistency matters across teams, AI outputs feed into other systems, and decisions carry financial or reputational risk.

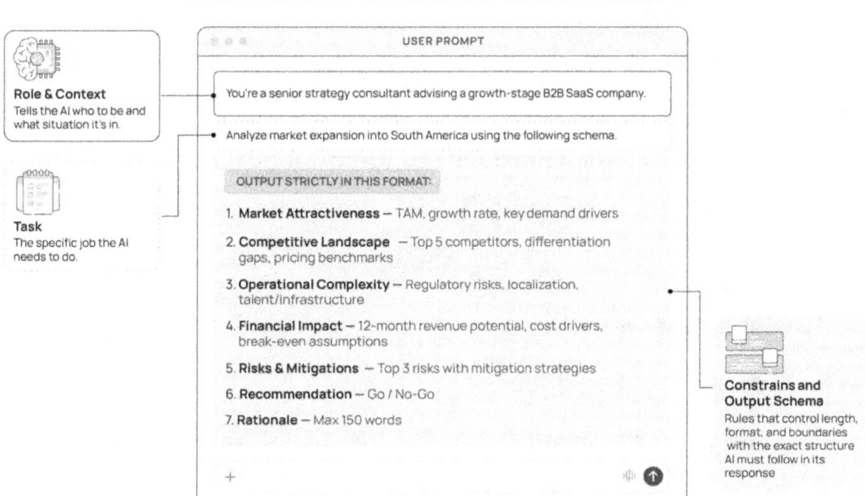

Context Compression

The context compression prompting technique involves distilling complex background information into its most decision-relevant elements before feeding it to the model. Rather than pasting long documents, transcripts, or datasets into a prompt, you summarize, prioritize, and structure the context so the AI receives only what materially affects the outcome. This matters because LLMs don't inherently know which details are important.

In business settings, more information doesn't always mean a better answer, but better information does. Therefore, from an executive standpoint, context compression mirrors how leaders operate. Board decks are curated narratives rather than raw data dumps. The same discipline must be applied when prompting AI. By compressing context, you guide the model's attention toward the variables that actually drive decisions: objectives, constraints, assumptions, and trade-offs.

Context compression is especially valuable in strategy, finance, and operations, where the source material is dense and time-sensitive. It improves speed, reduces error rates, and ensures that outputs remain aligned with the strategic question at hand. When combined with schema-first prompting, it creates a powerful pairing of clear inputs and predictable outputs. Consider the following example:

"You're advising a Series B SaaS company considering a price increase.

Compressed context:

- Current MRR: $450k
- Churn: 4.2% monthly (price-sensitive small and medium business [SMB] segment)
- Competitors charge 15–25% more for similar features
- Product differentiation: automation depth and onboarding speed

Using this context, evaluate whether a pricing increase is viable, and recommend a strategy using this structure: risks, mitigations, expected impact, and final recommendation."

Negative Prompting

Negative prompting means explicitly instructing an AI model on what it should avoid when generating output. This is like a strict constraint, but specifically on things you prohibit the model from doing. Think of the need to reiterate the irrelevant outputs the model should steer clear of after describing the prompt, context, and examples. In AI text generation, negative prompting is often used to control writing style and tone, improve relevance and accuracy, avoid redundancy, encourage creativity, and filter out bias and sensitivity.

Negative prompts can help you safeguard your brand integrity and compliance. Imagine a technology start-up integrating a system prompt instructing the model to avoid generating medical, legal, or financial advice to maintain regulatory standards. For example, you can say, "Explain crypto staking, but ignore price speculation or trading advice," and the output would still be domain-rich, minus the model acting as authorized personnel.

Negative prompting is often embedded in safety guardrails (see "Guarded Generation" below); however, there are some instances where you can use this technique for non-compliance topics. These include common negative prompting techniques you can experiment with right away, such as putting "-AI" at the end of your search queries to avoid AI-generated responses popping up. Another one is explicitly asking the model to avoid adding any extra limbs, distorted faces, blurry details, unwanted colors, or unnatural features to refine art in image generation. You can also ask AI to avoid changing any of your natural features when creating a digital twin. When doing research, you can ask the model to avoid citations that have no verifiable sources.

Guarded Generation

Guarded generation is a crucial concept in AI-driven content creation, especially for businesses seeking to maintain brand integrity, comply with regulations, and encourage positive customer engagement. It refers to the practice of deliberately controlling and constraining the output of generative AI models to avoid producing content that's inappropriate, harmful, misleading, or inconsistent with desired business values and goals. Guardrails ensure ethical AI, particularly in fields where misstatements, regulatory language, and liability matter.

As I mentioned above, there's a thin line between guarded generation and negative prompting, as not all constraints are ethics-related. However, there's a reason why the two work so cohesively. Negative prompting can be directly connected to guarded generation for specific topics. It involves specifying what should be avoided in the generated content, thereby guiding the AI away from unwanted themes, language, or styles. This technique is essential for businesses aiming to safeguard their reputation and prevent costly missteps in marketing, customer communications, product descriptions, or social media interactions.

For example, a fashion retailer using AI to generate promotional content might employ negative prompting within guarded generation to exclude any references to sensitive or controversial topics, such as political issues or body shaming. This ensures that all generated messages are aligned with the brand's inclusive and positive image. Similarly, a financial services company might guard against the generation of overly optimistic or unrealistic investment claims that could lead to regulatory issues, using negative prompting to filter out such language.

Integrating both guarded generation and negative prompting enables you to leverage the creative power of AI while mitigating the risks, ensuring that your AI-produced content remains professional, on-brand, and compliant with industry standards.

Delimiter-Based Prompts (Text Modification)

Delimiter-based prompting is an advanced technique for guiding AI to modify or generate text within clearly defined boundaries. This approach involves enclosing specific parts of the input text within unique delimiters—symbols or strings like brackets, quotation marks, or special characters—that signal to the model exactly where to focus its modifications or enhancements. Delimiter-based prompts enable you to precisely control which parts of your text the AI modifies, which can streamline communication and content creation for entrepreneurial success.

For entrepreneurs aiming to refine pitches, craft persuasive emails, or generate compelling marketing content, delimiter-based prompting helps to isolate key segments for targeted improvements. This ensures clarity and impact without unintentionally altering the core message. You can use these symbols to separate sections or parts of a prompt for clarity, emphasize or highlight important parts manually, or indicate placeholders or tags for insertion or special processing. Consider the following examples:

- **Email refinement:** "Improve the text between the brackets to make it more persuasive for potential investors: 'Dear Investor, [I am excited to share our groundbreaking product that will revolutionize the market and deliver exponential returns]. Thank you for your time.'"
- **Product description enhancement:** "Rewrite the content inside the curly braces to be more engaging and customer-focused: Our latest gadget offers {cutting-edge features and unbeatable performance} that help entrepreneurs save time and boost productivity."
- **Business mission statement clarification:** "Polish the mission statement section enclosed in parentheses for clarity and impact: Our company aims to (deliver innovative tech solutions that empower small businesses to scale rapidly) in competitive markets."

You can also use special characters, such as asterisks and hashtags, to separate and format sections within a lengthy prompt in Markdown language. For example, "Create a comprehensive business proposal for a new digital marketing strategy aimed at increasing brand awareness and customer engagement for a mid-sized ecommerce company. ### Executive Summary: Outline the main objectives, target audience, and expected outcomes of the strategy. ### Market Analysis: Provide insights into current market trends, competitor analysis, and customer demographics. ### Strategy Development: Detail the specific digital marketing tactics to be employed, including SEO, social media campaigns, email marketing, and influencer partnerships. ### Implementation Plan: Describe the timeline, resources required, team responsibilities, and budget allocation. ### Performance Metrics: Specify KPIs to measure the success of the strategy and methods for ongoing monitoring and adjustment."

While the effect of these symbols might vary based on the specific AI model or interface you're using, they're often the same across most LLMs. Delimiters are usually part of Markdown or JSON (industry standard) that you use when you want the model to grasp clear instructions, generate structured outputs, or organize data in a readable manner. The rule of thumb is to use industry-standard languages like JSON or XML and to avoid using symbols that interfere with your content, such as using quote delimiters within content that already contains quotation marks. If you aren't familiar with these, you can ask AI to guide you on common delimiters and how to use them.

In the example above, you're likely to get the output with level 3 headings (H3) for phrases starting with the triple hashtags (###). Asterisks indicate phrases you want bolded and italicized. Have you noticed how, when you press [ENTER] on your keyboard, the model goes on to generate a response even if you were simply trying to create a new paragraph within your prompt? Using symbols or delimiter prompts solves this problem if you want to skip creating prompts in a separate text-based tool.

Hybrid Prompting

Instead of opting for a specific prompt technique, stacking them might be essential to get a comprehensive output. For instance, you can combine few-shot, persona, schema-first, and CoT and add iterative refinement in one task. For example, "Here are three product landing pages (few-shot). Assume the role of a direct-response strategist (persona-driven). Think step-by-step (CoT) and rewrite for SaaS founders." Depending on the outcome and project needs, you can also leverage prompt chaining to extract more details and keep refining and adjusting until the final prompt yields a desired output.

Hybrid prompting is the next level of prompting that can promote any basic AI user to a prompt hero. You can use this method to create long-form content, ads, landing pages, investor decks, and onboarding flows. Nonetheless, this does not signify that hybrid prompting outperforms other techniques when used in isolation. Sometimes, a single technique suffices for a particular task, while some complex tasks might require a combination. The trick is analyzing the task in detail, considering its complexity and available resources, understanding the desired outcome, and selecting a befitting approach for optimum results.

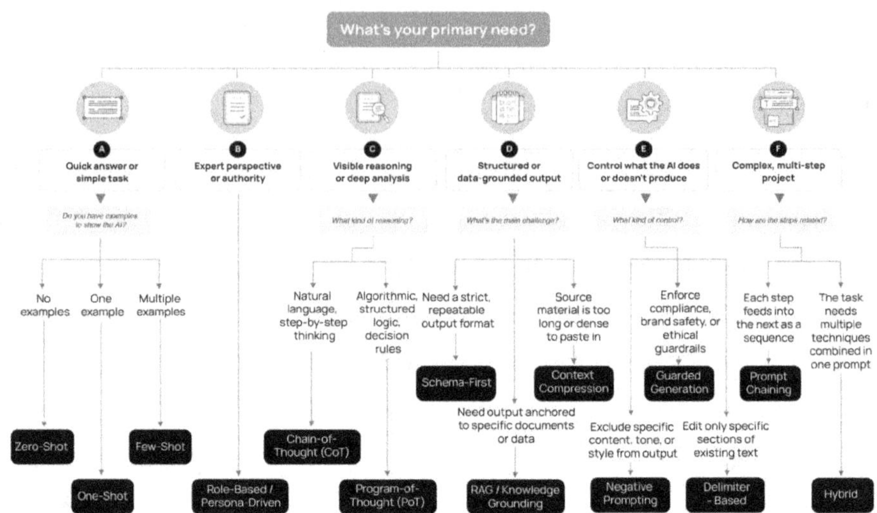

Practical Exercises

Let's get hands-on and experiment with these prompt techniques, individually or in combination, using any AI writing or chat platform. The following interactive exercises will build practical skills in crafting prompts and deepen understanding of how each advanced technique impacts AI behavior and results.

Exercise 1: Zero-Shot Prompting

- **Task:** Ask the AI to list five emerging technologies impacting your industry with no examples.
- **Goal:** Experience how the AI responds based solely on its general training.
- **Follow-up:** Modify the prompt to specify the format or order, and observe how it changes.

Exercise 2: One-Shot Prompting Format

- **Task:** Provide a single example of a product description with a specific tone and format. Then ask the AI to generate a similar description for a second product.
- **Goal:** Understand how one example influences output style and structure.

Exercise 3: Few-Shot Prompting

- **Task:** Create a prompt including three to four example data entries and request the AI to continue the list.
- **Goal:** See how giving multiple examples improves relevance and accuracy.
- **Variation:** Try different numbers of examples and compare results.

Exercise 4: Role-Based Prompting Scenario

- **Task:** Choose a professional role, such as CEO, marketer, or HR manager. Be specific when selecting a role for this task, whether it relates to your field or is relevant to a particular project. Remember, you can have numerous chats, so don't fear that changing a role will affect your entire settings. You have the option to clear chats and restart with another specific role for a different task. Write a prompt instructing the AI to respond as that role, providing full context.
- **Goal:** Practice crafting inputs that utilize persona-driven prompting.
- **Variation:** Ask the AI to switch roles and regenerate responses for comparison.

Exercise 5: CoT Reasoning

- **Task:** Prompt the AI, "Think step-by-step: What are the specific risks and benefits of remote work for a start-up in terms of productivity, team communication, company culture, employee satisfaction, operational costs, and scalability? After identifying these aspects, analyze how these risks can be mitigated and how the benefits can be fully leveraged to support the start-up's growth and success. Finally, suggest actionable strategies for implementing remote work policies effectively in a start-up environment."
- **Goal:** Encourage the AI to provide detailed reasoning rather than a surface answer.
- **Reflection:** Note how and where the AI breaks down reasoning.

Exercise 6: PoT Prompting

- **Task:** Ask the AI to "Write a detailed step-by-step algorithm for evaluating potential new suppliers. The evaluation should be based on three key criteria: cost, reliability, and delivery time. For each criterion, specify how to collect and analyze relevant data, how to establish benchmarks or thresholds for acceptable performance, and how to weigh those factors to make a final decision. Include considerations for trade-offs between the criteria, methods for verifying supplier information, and suggestions for documenting and comparing supplier evaluations comprehensively."
- **Goal:** Experience structured problem-solving outputs that mimic coding or workflows.

Exercise 7: Prompt Chaining

- **Task:** Break a complex problem into smaller parts. Example: "Analyze current sales data and identify trends." "Research competitor pricing strategies based on trend analysis." "Recommend pricing adjustments with reasons."
- **Goal:** Practice sequential prompting and iterative refinement.

Exercise 8: Schema-First Prompt Design

- **Task:** Create a prompt for a market entry analysis using a detailed schema with sections like Market Size, Competition, Challenges, and Recommendations.
- **Goal:** Learn how structuring prompts increases clarity and output usefulness.

Exercise 9: Context Compression

- **Task:** Summarize a complex business scenario into key facts and constraints, then prompt AI for strategic recommendations based on the compressed context.
- **Goal:** Practice distilling context for more relevant AI guidance.

Exercise 10: Negative Prompting Constraints

- **Task:** Write a prompt with explicit instructions on what to avoid. For example, "Explain blockchain technology without discussing cryptocurrencies."
- **Goal:** See how negative prompting controls content focus and relevance.

Exercise 11: Guarded Generation Scenario

- **Task:** Create a prompt to generate marketing content for a trendy makeup line, but instruct the model to avoid any controversial or sensitive topics (like race or gender).
- **Goal:** Practice safeguarded generation ensuring tone and compliance.

Exercise 12: Delimiter-Based Text Modification

- **Task:** Choose your preferred model and use delimiters, such as brackets, hashtags, or asterisks, to mark parts of a text for refinement or rewriting.
- **Example:** "Enrich the sentence in brackets by adding quantifiable metrics and descriptive language highlighting benefits, not just features to position the product above the competition: [Our product is **good** and **popular**.]"
- **Goal:** Get comfortable with guiding AI on sections to focus on.

Exercise 13: Hybrid Prompting

- **Task:** Combine methods by giving examples (few-shot), specifying a role, and asking for step-by-step reasoning in one prompt.
- **Goal:** Experiment with stacking techniques for complex outputs.

Key Takeaways

- Advanced prompting methods range from zero-shot (no examples) and few-shot (multiple examples) to role-based prompting, chain-of-thought reasoning, and program-of-thought prompting, each serving distinct purposes depending on task complexity.
- Retrieval-augmented generation (RAG) and knowledge grounding enhance AI accuracy by injecting external data sources into prompts, reducing hallucination and ensuring that responses are grounded in verified information.
- Schema-first design and context compression are powerful techniques for structuring complex prompts efficiently, enabling you to deliver more information within token limits while maintaining output quality.
- Negative prompting, guarded generation, and delimiter-based prompts give you precise control over AI output by specifying what to exclude, setting safety constraints, and marking text sections for targeted modifications.
- Hybrid prompting combines multiple techniques such as roles, constraints, chain-of-thought, and examples, into a single prompt to handle complex, multifaceted tasks that no single method can address effectively.

CHAPTER

HOW TO BE PRODUCTIVE AND EFFICIENT WITH AI

Throughout the AI frenzy, productivity and efficiency have long separated average performers from category leaders. Top executives who multiply their output don't log more hours but build smarter systems that make it easier to delegate work, automate processes, and create decision frameworks. Fortunately, AI is now delivering the biggest leverage leap since the advent of spreadsheets, the internet, and cloud computing. You don't have to be a Fortune 500 company to 10× your productivity, because AI gives everyone willing to learn and deploy its power a competitive edge.

This chapter focuses on how AI can increase productivity through automated workflows, leveraging AI tools, and the power of effective prompting. It delivers practical, real-world business examples, repeatable systems, and actionable prompts to turn AI into a superpowered force and collaborative partner that amplifies your time management, communication, content creation, decision-making, and execution.

AI-Powered Productivity

One of the core areas where AI truly shines is increasing productivity and efficiency. You've probably heard how this technology can free up time spent on repetitive and mundane tasks, allowing humans to focus more on strategic and high-impact work. Recent research reveals that about 60% of all occupations have at least 30% automation potential (Saji, 2025).

Automate Your Calendar

Manually updating your calendar one entry at a time may seem like a low-effort task—until you're bombarded with time-sensitive entries that require precision and accuracy to avoid double bookings or missing important activities. Appointment scheduling and calendar management tools are some of the common AI integrations that boost efficiency and productivity.

Most AI-driven calendar tools can schedule meetings around priorities and optimal focus times, dynamically adjusting as priorities shift throughout the week. Top tools, such as Clockwise, Lindy, Motion, Calendly, and Clara, not only schedule and coordinate meetings but also have agentic abilities to handle multiple duties and streamline your workflows. They can even integrate time blocking and habits tracking to improve work–life balance.

You can deploy an AI scheduling assistant to automatically handle meeting invites, prioritize focus blocks for deep work, and minimize context-switching. After creating a free account on any of the tools above, you can add dummy or existing calendar entries and use the following prompt: "Review my calendar for the upcoming week. Prioritize time blocks for strategic projects, and auto-reschedule conflicts or low-priority meetings." This enables you to start each week knowing what to focus on rather than spending hours coordinating meetings and juggling activities. You can also use agent mode in ChatGPT and link your Google (or any other) calendar.

Pro tip: The only way you'll see results is if you actually add stuff to your calendar. You can ask any LLM to suggest items that need to be in your calendar; you'll see how you often omit some "near-automatic tasks" that are obvious to you, such that you don't need a reminder. Your AI calendar assistant needs all that information to be effective. If you don't want to explicitly label the activity, you can mark it as busy or give it a pseudonym. Just don't leave it blank.

Email Management

Email management continues to be a critical aspect of productivity for entrepreneurs and professionals alike. According to a 2012 McKinsey report, at that time, knowledge workers were allocating approximately 28% of their workweek to repetitive tasks ripe for automation, with email management being a major component (Chui et al., 2012). Fast-forward to today, and advancements in AI-driven email automation tools have transformed how entrepreneurs handle their inboxes, enhancing both efficiency and effectiveness.

Modern email automation AI apps such as Superhuman, SaneBox, and Spike leverage machine learning algorithms to triage incoming emails by priority and sender importance, significantly reducing the time spent on sorting. These AI tools also personalize draft responses by analyzing the user's historical communication style, enabling you to quickly reply to emails with relevant, context-aware messages. Clean

Email uses AI to group similar emails, making it easier to unsubscribe, archive, or delete bulk emails in one click. Additionally, integrated AI assistants, such as Google's Smart Compose and Microsoft's Outlook AI, can automatically suggest responses and detect when follow-ups or reminders should be sent; this helps you stay on top of crucial deadlines without manual intervention.

Leveraging the latest AI email automation tools enables you to reclaim valuable hours, ensure prompt communication, and maintain a competitive edge in business through smarter email management. You can benefit from these AI email management solutions by gaining more time to focus on strategic tasks and business growth rather than mundane inbox maintenance. These tools also improve client relationships by ensuring timely and professional responses, minimizing missed opportunities and miscommunications. Moreover, using AI to flag urgent emails or important proposals ensures critical messages never get buried under less important correspondence.

Prompt: "Sort my inbox by client priority and flag emails requiring urgent responses. Draft a professional follow-up for last week's pending proposals, maintaining my typical formal tone but adding a polite urgency."

Meeting Management

Since 2020, with the rise of remote and hybrid work, workers are spending more time in meetings than ever before: up to 11.3 hours per week for an average employee (Teter, 2025). While this may be lower for leaders than for knowledge workers, the overall time spent in meetings can affect high-impact activities within the organization, especially when those meetings occur during early productive hours. Further research revealed that 35% of meetings are a waste of time and resources (The London School of Economics and Political Science, 2024). From agenda preparation to invitations, note-taking, and report generation, several activities can be automated to reclaim productivity time. Whether meetings occur in-person or virtually, automating these activities can reduce the time they take up tremendously.

With readily available meeting management and productivity tools, such as Fathom, Fireflies, Notta, and Avoma, you can now get more from online meetings and collect important data from webinars. These tools can easily integrate with popular meeting apps, like Zoom Meetings, Google Meet, and Microsoft Teams. Some of these virtual assistants can track your calendar, log into meetings earlier if you're running late, and start taking notes on your behalf. You can even ask if your name was mentioned before your arrival and get a follow-up on any prior requests.

In addition, AI can help you with agenda creation, meeting transcription, note-taking, real-time summarization, action-item extraction, follow-up drafts, and auto-assigning action items to task teams, making shorter meetings feasible and actionable.

Leveraging effective prompt techniques from the previous chapters, you can ask AI to help you with a strategy to save your organization time and manage meetings better.

Optimized Administrative Work

Optimizing administrative tasks is crucial for maintaining operational efficiency and gaining a competitive edge. AI technologies excel at automating repetitive and time-consuming processes such as data entry standardization, invoice triage, HR screening, and customer ticket prioritization. By leveraging these capabilities, you can propel your team to new productivity heights and transform your entire workflow into a streamlined, well-oiled machine.

One effective approach involves combining LLMs for intelligent classification and data extraction with low-code automation platforms like Zapier, Make, n8n, or Power Automate. This combination enables the seamless transfer of structured outputs directly into downstream applications such as CRM systems, accounting software, or HR management platforms. For example, in an invoice triage process, an AI-powered LLM can automatically classify invoices by type, extract relevant financial data, and trigger tailored workflows to notify the right departments for approval, reducing manual errors and speeding up payment cycles.

A prompt like "Classify incoming customer support tickets by urgency and product type, extract essential details such as customer ID and issue description, and create prioritized task entries in our helpdesk system" can facilitate faster response times, improved customer satisfaction, and enhanced overall team productivity. This strategic application of AI and automation tools ultimately drives operational excellence and frees your staff to focus on higher-value activities.

If you don't want to rely on any specific automation tool, since newer ones are emerging at an exponential rate, you can design your own optimized workflow by creating a project within any preferred GPT. All you need to do is upload your files (CSV, customer tickets, etc.) as the knowledge base for the model and ask it to suggest an automated workflow process using the prompting techniques we discussed in the previous chapter.

Content Creation and Thought Leadership

From proposals to reports, marketing copy, client emails, legal drafts, and social media posts, leveraging AI to streamline content creation and establish thought leadership is a game-changer. Imagine you want to develop a comprehensive and versatile content calendar that includes social media posts, email campaigns, blog articles, and thought leadership pieces. The objective is to align all content with your company's quarterly business goals to maximize impact and engagement.

Prompt: "You're a top creative writer for [COMPANY/INDUSTRY]. Create a weekly content plan focused on product benefits, customer testimonials, and industry trends for Q3 with actionable CTAs."

This prompt guides the AI to generate content ideas that blend promotional messaging with educational elements to nurture leads and build trust within the target market. A pro tip is to turn the AI into an assistant by setting a strict brief, providing a revision checklist, and saving iterations as templates.

For example, a SaaS company aiming to boost user acquisition in Q3 might receive a calendar with posts highlighting easy-to-use features of their software, success stories from satisfied customers, and insights on the evolving tech landscape relevant to their industry. The AI model can suggest email subject lines that drive open rates, blog article titles that establish thought leadership, and LinkedIn post ideas encouraging community interaction. Additionally, each piece of content would include a clear CTA, such as signing up for a demo, downloading a case study, or joining a webinar.

You can also use AI to help you with first drafts of long-form written content and ask human editors to review instead of writing from scratch.

Prompt: "You're a proposal writer specializing in [INDUSTRY]. Create a two-page proposal for [CLIENT] offering [SOLUTION]. Include a problem statement, approach (three phases), timeline, pricing model (high-level), and three success metrics. Use a professional persuasive tone."

Data Synthesis and Insights

The Internet of Things (IoT) and AI have made information synthesis and research critical capabilities in today's fast-paced business environment, significantly reducing the time spent on data gathering and analysis. This is invaluable in various scenarios such as market scans, regulatory summaries, literature reviews, and competitive intelligence. Advanced AI technologies enable organizations and professionals to efficiently digest vast volumes of text, extracting core themes and producing well-structured summaries or briefing decks. This process facilitates faster decision-making cycles and enables more informed CTAs, translating into tangible business advantages.

Some of the high-ranking AI tools making strides in data analysis include Claude, Outskill AI Mastermind, Julius AI, and Quadratic. These tools can synthesize data, break it down into graphs and charts, include summaries, and even allow you to run code without the need for a specialized integrated development environment (IDE). One way to identify the best data analytics AI tools is their easy integration with tools you already use, such as Excel, Tableau, and Power BI. You can upload data files into these tools, which will analyze them and provide key insights instantly without moving data across platforms.

For example, let's say you upload a collection of PDFs and meeting notes into a retrieval-augmented AI agent. By requesting a concise one-page executive brief combined with three recommended actions, you can decrease your preparation time significantly. This time saving empowers you to focus more on stakeholder engagement and strategic alignment rather than data synthesis. The AI-driven approach turns complex and unstructured information into actionable insights, improving both efficiency and decision quality.

Prompt: "You're an expert analyst. Read the following documents [FILE LIST]. Produce:

1. A 250-word executive summary that captures the key themes and conclusions.
2. The top five emerging trends with supporting evidence (including quotes and sources).
3. Three strategic implications ranked by urgency.
4. Two suggested next steps, complete with designated owners and timelines."

This ensures the output is targeted and relevant, enabling leadership to swiftly understand the critical issues, anticipate market movements, and prioritize initiatives accordingly.

It's worth reiterating that human oversight is not an option but a necessary precaution to ensure the accuracy of the AI-generated content. A scandal recently blew up in Deloitte Australia's face after AI messed up a government report with fake citations, non-existent references, and fabricated quotes. A blunder of that magnitude not only came with reputational cost, but the Australian government also ordered Deloitte to pay a partial refund of A$440,00 (roughly $290,000) (Tadros & Karp, 2025). This highlights the importance of verifying every AI-generated output, especially when working with sensitive content or data insights.

Coding and Technical Work

GitHub developers reported 75% improved job satisfaction and 55% faster coding (without compromising code quality) through Copilot integration (Wrótniak, 2025). AI-powered coding assistants, such as code completion tools, bug triage systems, unit test generators, and automated documentation creators, streamline the development process by reducing manual effort and enabling developers to focus on higher-value tasks.

Practically, AI reduces the number of keystrokes and time spent writing repetitive or boilerplate code, which traditionally consumes a substantial portion of developers' workdays. By providing intelligent code suggestions and examples, these assistants help developers avoid common pitfalls and expedite the implementation of complex features.

For junior engineers, AI accelerates onboarding by offering tailored code snippets and context-aware explanations, thereby flattening the learning curve and integrating them more quickly into project workflows.

A 25% boost in AI usage corresponds to a 2.1% increase in productivity, demonstrating how AI can enhance the daily work of developers. Moreover, developers have noted enhancements in key aspects like workflow productivity and code generation speed (Shani & GitHub Staff, 2024).

In a business context, integrating AI-driven coding assistants can translate into faster time-to-market, lower development costs, and improved product quality, empowering software teams to innovate with greater agility and confidence. GitHub Copilot, Windsurf, Cursor, and Gemini in Android Studio are some of the best coding assistants.

These AI tools enhance code quality by flagging potential bugs early and automating unit test generation, which boosts reliability and reduces downstream maintenance efforts. However, the human element remains critical. Developers must review AI-generated outputs meticulously to ensure correctness, maintain security standards, and uphold codebase integrity.

You can experiment with the following prompt example: "Enhance our software development team's productivity by integrating an AI-powered coding assistant that automates code completion, bug triage, unit test generation, and documentation. Ensure the solution provides context-aware suggestions to accelerate onboarding for junior developers while maintaining high standards for code quality and security compliance."

Here's where it gets interesting: You can actually build technical applications, such as websites, client portals, CRMs, or even entire SaaS businesses, without writing a single line of code, thanks to zero-code AI tools. Lovable, Base44, Hostinger Horizons, Bubble, and v0 are some of the best platforms that non-coders can leverage to complete technical projects that previously required coding. Not only do these app builders come with customizable templates, but you can also easily integrate them with other applications via APIs, import designs, and quickly set them up (with workflow automations) for fast prototyping.

For instance, you can type your idea into Base44 and see it come to life in minutes by using this prompt: "I'm building a network marketing platform [or any idea] for [INDUSTRY/COMPANY] with a visible downline builder to reflect direct referrals, genealogies, cycling milestones, and bonuses. Create this using the following brand kit or palette [PASTE EXISTING VISUALS OR GIVE IT CREATIVE FREEDOM AND MODIFY AS NEEDED]." If you want to see the ideation process, you can ask, "Help me build it step-by-step by asking me about things you require to make this the best platform teams can use to generate and follow up on their leads and rank up." Most AI-powered app builders allow you to modify your prompts based on output or by using their suggested prompts to take your idea further.

Practical Exercises

The following exercises will help you to gradually build expertise with AI tools and promote the adoption of AI-powered productivity practices throughout your business operations. You can set up one AI tool weekly to automate recurring tasks from email sorting to report generation; the goal is to experiment with these tools and track your productivity. You can also experiment with the different AI prompts discussed in the previous chapters and refine them based on output quality.

- Identify three repetitive tasks in your daily workflow that take up the most time.
- **Automate your calendar:** Select an AI calendar assistant like Clockwise or Calendly. Set it up to manage your meetings for one week, using a prompt to prioritize strategic projects and reschedule conflicts.

- **Email management:** Connect an AI email management tool like SaneBox to your inbox. Use a prompt to sort emails by priority and draft responses for at least five emails. Track how much time you save.
- **Meeting management:** Use a meeting assistant tool like Fathom or Avoma in your next three meetings. Employ AI to generate agendas, take notes, and extract action items. Review AI-generated summaries for accuracy and completeness.
- **Optimized administrative work:** Choose one administrative workflow, such as invoice processing or customer support ticketing. Create a simple AI prompt to classify and prioritize tasks, then integrate it with an automation platform like Zapier for one week.
- **Content creation:** Use an AI content creation tool to build a one-week content calendar aligned with your current business goals. Then, generate a draft of a key content piece using AI, and revise it before publishing.
- **Data synthesis and insights:** Gather recent documents or data relevant to your business. Upload them into an AI analytics tool and request a summary with strategic implications and next steps. Plan actions based on AI insights.
- **Coding and technical work:** If applicable, explore an AI coding assistant like GitHub Copilot or Cursor. Have it generate code snippets or automated tests for a small project task. Review the AI-produced code for quality and compliance. You can also explore Lovable or Base44 to create a zero-code website or app and customize it as you wish.
- **General productivity:** Schedule a daily "AI productivity hour" for one week, dedicating that time to experimenting

with AI-generated outputs on high-leverage projects. Record improvements in workflow efficiency.

- **Bonus exercise (self-assessment):** List all the tools, platforms, and methods you've explored so far. How have you improved your productivity? Did you see visible time- or money-saving results? Is there a way you can improve your strategy to work smarter? Document it. Outline tools you want to keep in your playbook, and commit to exploring them further.

Key Takeaways

- AI-powered productivity tools can automate calendar management, email triage, meeting summaries, and administrative tasks, freeing up significant time for high-value strategic work.
- Content creation and thought leadership can be accelerated with AI by drafting reports, articles, presentations, and social media content, then refining the output with human expertise and brand voice.
- AI excels at data synthesis and insight generation, helping professionals analyze large datasets, identify patterns, and make data-driven decisions faster than manual analysis allows.
- Coding and technical work can be significantly streamlined with AI assistants that help write, debug, refactor, and document code, making technical tasks more accessible even to non-developers.
- The key to AI-powered productivity is using specific, well-crafted prompts with clear objectives, constraints, and context rather than treating AI as a simple search engine.

Are You Finding This Book Valuable?

I'd Love to Hear from You!

Your feedback makes a world of difference, not only to me as a new author, but also to other people seeking to unlock the value of AI in their lives.

If this book brought you insights, inspiration, or important information, would you have just 2 minutes to spare to share your thoughts?

Your review helps me create even better resources for you and helps others discover this valuable guide.

Whether it's a quick note or a detailed response, every piece of feedback counts and is deeply appreciated.

Thank you for supporting this journey!

CHAPTER

HOW TO DEVELOP YOUR CREATIVITY AND INNOVATION

While AI may not possess vision or independent creative discretion, it can significantly amplify your creativity when carefully guided or given curated artistic instructions. Together, thanks to AI's generative capabilities, you can collaborate to craft a masterpiece. Behind the scenes, generative models analyze vast amounts of data to recognize patterns, generate novel combinations, and simulate human-like creativity through complex algorithms and neural networks.

Understanding how AI functions internally allows you to manipulate prompts more effectively, moving beyond basic tips to fully harness AI's potential. You can prompt a model to think artistically, perhaps even like Leonardo da Vinci or another renowned artist, and it embodies the specified character to unleash that level of creative ability. Whether you're tasking it to brainstorm for a masterpiece you're creating or want it to go ahead and bring your idea to life, great prompting is how AI comprehends your instructions and delivers your desired output.

This chapter explores how AI serves as a thinking and creative partner to overcome creative blocks, stress-test ideas, enhance ideation quality, and swiftly transition from concept to execution. Today's AI tools empower you to challenge assumptions, uncover overlooked possibilities, and propose limitless alternatives.

Ideation and Brainstorming

While many are still arguing about whether AI-generated and AI-assisted art deserves merit, forward-thinking leaders are leveraging the technology to create masterpieces in half the time. With clarity, precision, speed, and the ability to imagine out-of-this-world things, generative AI enables creators to take their creativity to the next level. As a prompting hero with advanced techniques, there are no limits to what you can create with AI. AI-powered tools, such as ChatGPT,

Claude, and Gemini, can turbocharge ideation and brainstorming sessions, helping you to unlock new perspectives, generate disruptive ideas, and refine concepts precisely.

Disruptive Thinking

Disruption often fails because teams optimize existing models instead of challenging underlying assumptions. AI can systematically surface non-obvious alternatives by breaking pattern lock-in. You can challenge conventional paradigms by prompting AI models to generate out-of-the-box perspectives. Through effective prompting, AI models can suggest unconventional business models that could disrupt any industry, giving you a competitive advantage. You can unlock unlimited imagination and prompt AI to generate innovative ideas that have never been tried before, then marvel at the output.

Prompt: "Assume our current approach to an urban mobility app for commuters is fundamentally flawed. List 10 radically different ways in which this problem could be solved if cost was irrelevant, regulations didn't exist, commuters were completely different, and technology was 10× more powerful."

Strategy teams exploring new business models and founders stress-testing core assumptions can highly benefit from using AI in this manner.

Challenging Idea Framing

The quality of ideas depends heavily on how problems are framed. AI is effective at reframing challenges into clearer, more generative questions. You can use AI to evaluate ideas and frame challenges that push boundaries critically.

Prompt: "Rewrite the problem of low adoption of our urban mobility app in five different ways: as a customer pain point, a cost problem, a growth opportunity, a systems failure, and a behavioral challenge."

Diversified Brainstorming

To avoid the common groupthink that comes with traditional brainstorming, you can prompt AI to incorporate cross-industry insights and simulate diverse viewpoints. For instance, weaving guardrails and ethics into any AI project prompts AI to work across multiple industries. This is because AI enables parallel ideation across cognitive styles, personas, and industries.

Prompt: "Generate improvement ideas for our urban mobility app from the perspectives of a venture capitalist, a daily commuter, a city transport official, a customer who hates our app, and a competitor trying to replace us."

This technique reliably increases idea variance, which correlates with higher innovation quality.

Concept Enhancement

You may recall prompt enhancing and refining from earlier chapters (iterative refinement). You can start with a basic prompt or concept and refine it based on the output. AI can enrich or expand your initial concept to add depth and clarity or to change perspective.

Prompt: "Take this rough idea—an AI-powered commuter subscription that adapts routes in real time—and expand it into a clear value proposition. Include use cases, risks, constraints, failure points, and ways in which it could be made 10× better."

Scenario Exploration

You can also use AI to explore futuristic business scenarios to prepare strategic responses.

Prompt: "Create three future scenarios for urban mobility over the next five years: optimistic, pessimistic, and disruptive. Explain the strategic implications for our app in each scenario."

Trend Synthesis

Keeping up with the latest trends, news, and social chatter is a nightmare for any professional. Luckily, AI can synthesize trends into coherent narratives and enable you to stay ahead of your competitors and anticipate customer demands. You can stay ahead by asking AI to combine emerging trends into actionable business opportunities.

Prompt: "Synthesize how AI, IoT, and 5G could reshape urban commuting. Identify five emerging trends, why they matter, second-order implications, and risks if ignored."

Experiment With Different Brainstorming Techniques

Elevate your brainstorming and ideation sessions by deploying varied AI-supported techniques. Experiment with mind mapping, reverse thinking, or SCAMPER (Substitute, Combine, Adapt, Modify, Put to another use, Eliminate, Reverse) to unlock fresh perspectives and innovative solutions tailored to your business challenges:

- **Mind mapping:** Create a visual web of ideas around a central business concept or problem. This technique helps you explore all related aspects and their connections, leading to comprehensive solutions. **Prompt:** "Generate a mind map of potential customer segments, partnerships, and revenue streams for our urban mobility app."
- **Reverse thinking:** Challenge conventional ideas by considering the opposite approach or outcome. This can reveal hidden opportunities or risks that you might not have considered. **Prompt:** "What would happen if we stopped promoting convenience and instead marketed inconvenience as a feature? List possible insights."
- **SCAMPER:** Use this acronym to systematically innovate existing products, services, or processes. **Prompt:** "Apply SCAMPER to our current commuter rewards system to increase daily engagement and retention."

Experimenting with these techniques enables your business to cultivate a richer pool of ideas and strategies, helping you stay agile and competitive in a dynamic market.

The SCAMPER model

Seven perspectives to provoke creative solutions to challenging problems.

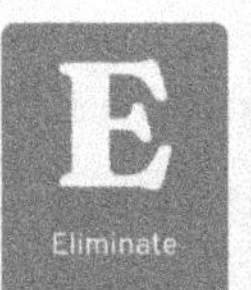

Substitute	Combine	Adapt	Modify	Put to another use	Eliminate	Reverse
Replace a part, material, or process with something else.	Join elements, ideas, or functions together in new ways – or find a new element you can merge with.	Modify something to better suit a new purpose, person or context.	Enlarge, reduce, change the shape, or alter attributes. Can a small change have a big effect?	Rather than changing the thing itself, consider changing the context it exists in.	Remove elements, simplify, or pare down to essentials. Is less more?	Flip the script, re-order your priorities, invert cause and effect, and turn it all upside-down.

BiteSize Learning

Ask for Specific Formats

We've already established that AI performs better when given explicit output structures. Instruct it to provide output in your preferred format (table, PDF, HTML, Markdown, etc.) to save you from editing.

Prompt: "Present the final recommendations for our urban mobility app as a comparison table with benefits, risks, and implementation effort."

Overcoming Creative Block

Contrary to the common belief that creative block arises from a lack of ideas, it's often the result of having an overwhelming and unstructured flood of ideas. In a business context, this overload can manifest during brainstorming sessions for new product development, marketing campaigns, or strategic planning. When faced with a blank page or an incoherent draft, the inability to organize and prioritize ideas can cause teams or individuals to feel stuck and unproductive. This is where AI can be a game-changer by helping to overcome creative block through its unique ability to impose order, add contrast, and introduce movement to the ideation process.

AI tools analyze patterns in your input, identify thematic connections, and highlight gaps or inconsistencies in your draft. For example, if you're drafting a business proposal or developing a brand narrative, AI can help by summarizing key points, suggesting logical sections, or reorganizing content flow to improve clarity and impact. This structured approach turns an overwhelming jumble of ideas into a clear, purposeful message.

To leverage AI effectively in overcoming creative block, consider these prompts:

- **Ask AI to structure your ideas:** "Here are my messy thoughts [PASTE]. Organize them into core themes, supporting ideas, gaps, and contradictions." "Help me organize these brainstorming notes for a new marketing strategy into a coherent outline with key themes."

- **Use the problem inversion technique to determine what not to do:** "If our goal was to completely fail at [OBJECTIVE], what actions would guarantee failure? Now, invert those into principles to follow." "What would be the opposite of our current business challenge, and how can reversing this perspective help us discover new solutions?"
- **Ask "what if" questions:** "What if we had to solve this problem with 50% fewer resources, no digital tools, a completely different customer, and/or a 24-hour deadline?"
- **Request metaphors to enhance communication:** "Suggest compelling metaphors that illustrate the value of our product to potential customers." "Explain [PROBLEM] using metaphors from nature, sports, warfare, or music."

Problem-Solving

Problem-solving is a critical skill in any department, and using AI enables organizations to overcome challenges, improve processes, and drive innovation more quickly. AI can bridge the gap between the problem and the solution. If you want to tackle challenges thoughtfully, systematically, and creatively to drive sustainable growth and innovation, integrating the following AI-powered problem-solving methodologies and prompts is key.

Identify the Problem

Clearly define the issue affecting your business and ask AI to identify where you're losing the plot. "Given this situation [DESCRIBE], identify the core problem, symptoms vs. root causes, and problems we may be misdiagnosing." Or if you know part of the problem, you can provide a bit of context using a prompt like this: "What are the main factors contributing to declining customer satisfaction in our retail stores?"

Discover New Perspectives

Encourage AI to give you diverse viewpoints to gain fresh insights into a situation. For example, "How might different departments perceive the bottleneck in our supply chain?"

Play Devil's Advocate

You can also explicitly ask AI to argue the proposed solution as someone with a strongly different opinion to highlight any hidden risks and assumptions. For instance, "What could go wrong if we implemented this new marketing strategy without further testing?"

Root Cause Analysis

AI can dig deep to uncover the underlying causes of a problem. For example, "What are the fundamental reasons behind the recent increase in product defects?"

Design Thinking

Task AI to focus on user-centered solutions by incorporating empathy and iterative prototyping. AI can help you generate detailed personas based on all the information you provide about your product, market, demographics, and more. These personas serve as realistic representations of your target users, allowing you to design solutions tailored to their specific needs.

Furthermore, you can use AI to test these solutions by asking it to role-play the personas, simulating their responses and feedback. This approach enhances your ability to empathize with users and refine your designs effectively.

Prompt: "Develop a group of personas that best represent our target customers based on all you know about our product/service [ATTACH KNOWLEDGE BASE]. Next, test the proposed solutions against the generated personas to ensure alignment with user needs."

Follow-up prompt: "Based on all you know about our personas, what would be your strategy when redesigning our mobile app to meet the needs of these personas? Please explain in detail the reasons behind your suggestions."

SWOT Analysis

Problem-solving also involves evaluating strengths, weaknesses, opportunities, and threats to devise a strategy. You can prompt AI to conduct a SWOT analysis for any initiative and then ask it to suggest strategic moves based on that analysis. For example, "What internal strengths and external opportunities can we leverage to enter a new market?"

Lean Six Sigma

This is a combination of waste elimination and variation reduction to improve business processes. AI can apply data-driven methods to reduce waste and improve quality.

Prompt: "Analyze the attached process steps [ATTACHMENT] and point out which ones are causing delays in order fulfillment and can be optimized for efficiency."

Plan–Do–Check–Act Cycle

Use ongoing, iterative cycles to improve operations continually. Ask AI to apply the plan–do–check–act (PDCA) cycle to enhance processes:

1. **Plan:** Develop strategies for improvement and define clear, measurable objectives.

2. **Do:** Implement small-scale trials of the new process or protocol.
3. **Check:** Analyze data and metrics to evaluate the effectiveness of the changes.
4. **Act:** Refine and standardize successful improvements for full-scale adoption.

Prompt: "How can we design a pilot test for a new customer service protocol, determine key performance metrics, and measure its impact before a full rollout?"

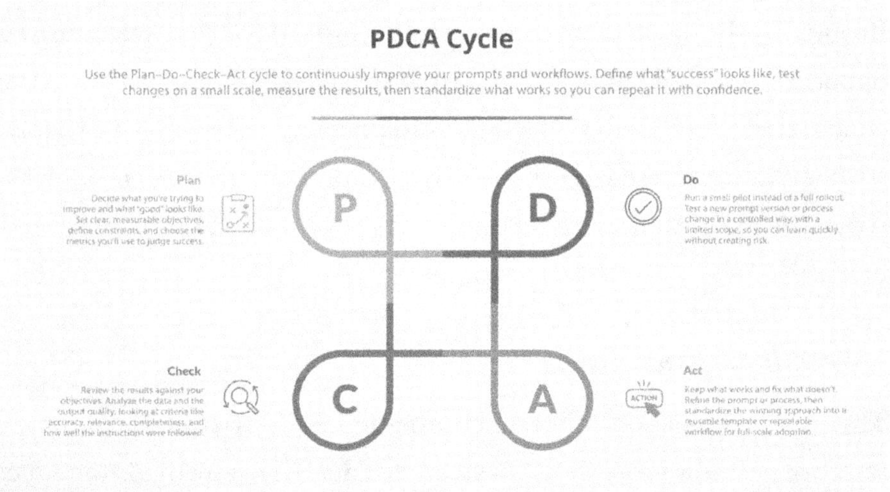

Six Thinking Hats

AI can apply parallel thinking to explore issues from different perspectives, like emotions, facts, and creativity. Consider the following prompt example: "Analyze this decision [SITUATION] using the Six Thinking Hats framework and provide insights under each hat." If you know which specific aspects the AI must focus on, explicitly ask, "What are the emotional and factual responses to our recent product launch?"

Ishikawa (Fishbone) Framework

The Ishikawa (fishbone) framework is a visual tool used to identify, explore, and display possible causes of a specific problem or effect. It resembles a fish's skeleton, with the "head" representing the problem and the "bones" that branch off representing categories of potential causes. This framework helps teams systematically analyze the factors contributing to an issue, making it easier to pinpoint root causes. You can prompt AI to visualize cause-and-effect relationships to organize potential problem causes.

Prompts: "Create a detailed and clear fishbone diagram illustrating the cause-and-effect relationships for [PROBLEM]. The diagram should show the main problem at the head and include categorized branches for causes such as people, processes, equipment, materials, environment, and management, with specific detailed causes labeled on each branch."

"Use the Ishikawa analysis for [PROBLEM] and indicate factors related to manpower, methods, materials, and machinery that could be influencing our production downtime."

Theory of Inventive Problem-Solving

Theory of inventive problem-solving (TRIZ) is a systematic methodology that uses inventive principles to overcome contradictions and innovate.

Prompt: "Apply TRIZ principles to resolve a contradiction: [DESCRIBE TRADE-OFF]." For instance, "How might we improve product durability without increasing manufacturing costs?"

Maintain Critical Human Oversight

To remain accountable for decisions (especially considering ethical and practical soundness), it's imperative to always ask humans to review, contextualize, and stress-test AI-generated analysis. You can't just copy and paste results from a prompt and call it a day. AI models have disclaimers, such as "AI can make errors," in fine print. Therefore, you must be aware of hallucinations, compliance risks, and other errors before using AI-generated results. There's a difference between using AI as a replacement and using it as a partner. Opt for the latter, and work collaboratively with AI to form a formidable fusion. That's what makes you a prompting hero.

Content Drafting and Editing

Generative AI has revolutionized how individuals and large organizations approach content creation and refinement, driving both creativity and innovation. Today, numerous AI-powered tools enable professionals to produce high-quality, impactful content quickly while maintaining consistency and brand voice.

Content Writing

AI systems can generate diverse types of business content tailored to specific industries and audiences. From crafting compelling marketing copy and persuasive sales proposals to drafting executive summaries and annual reports, AI accelerates content production without sacrificing quality. For example, a business launching new products can use AI to draft promotional blogs and social media posts aligned with the brand's key messaging and value propositions. Marketing teams can draft campaign copy and value propositions tailored to buyer personas, consultants can generate executive summaries and analytical narratives from raw research, and sales teams can create standardized but personalized outreach messaging at scale.

One of the most powerful features of LLMs is their capability to do deep research. When you start a new search on a model, you can click where it says "Deep Research" or "Thinking Mode" depending on the LLM. This allows the model to gather knowledge from hundreds of research sources, providing well-informed insights that enrich the content creation process. The free version of ChatGPT offers limited usage of deep research, while other LLMs, such as Perplexity, require a subscription to access this mode. Gemini has different thinking modes for free and pro version users. Leveraging this depth of research, content can be made more accurate, comprehensive, and authoritative.

It's worth noting that AI can fabricate sources to yield output that seems research-rich. Therefore, you must always verify facts and citations or ask the model to provide only verifiable research with links. To avoid fabricated citations when writing sensitive content, NotebookLM enables you to choose specific sources in different formats (URL, text, audio, or video files) to establish a guided knowledge base for your output.

Other top AI-powered content writing tools include ChatGPT, Claude, Perplexity, Gemini, and DeepSeek. WriteSonic, Jasper, and Copy.ai are top-rated tools for business writing workflows, including email marketing and copywriting. Notion AI and Writer.com are mostly preferred for contextual writing within documents and editorial workflows. Dibbly's Content Writer and KIP (in-text and chatbot) are ideal for professional manuscripts, blog posts, and SEO article writing, with the option to collaborate with a human ghostwriter and editor to ensure quality.

Prompts:

- "You're a professional business writer. Produce a structured draft report on [TOPIC]. Include an executive summary (three paragraphs), key findings from credible and verifiable sources (cited in APA style), strategic recommendations, and risks and mitigation. Use a formal business tone."

- "Write five personalized outreach email templates for [NICHE/INDUSTRY SEGMENT]. Each one should include a unique opening based on company context, a specific value proposition, and a concise CTA."

Proofreading and Editing

In addition to content writing, many AI tools offer advanced proofreading and editing capabilities that go beyond simple punctuation and spell checks. They identify context-based errors, suggest improvements to sentence clarity, enhance tone appropriateness, and ensure adherence to corporate style guides. This can help you maintain professionalism across all communication channels, including emails, client presentations, and internal reports.

Recent research indicates that human editors and proofreaders are also actively using AI-powered tools, reporting benefits such as time savings and enhanced text quality (Al Sawi & Alaa, 2024). AI tools significantly reduce the time editors spend on surface-level corrections while improving consistency and quality.

Grammar and Punctuation

Grammar and punctuation support credibility and thought leadership, especially in client-facing or regulated industries. AI grammar checkers and editors catch and eliminate errors that humans might overlook under deadline pressure. These tools provide real-time suggestions on verb tense consistency, subject–verb agreement, and punctuation use, helping to ensure precision and clarity in complex documents like contracts or compliance reports.

Grammarly and QuillBot are among the most common editing and proofreading tools. They're ideal for real-time proofreading, style and tone suggestions, paraphrasing, clarity optimization, and consistency checking. With tailored prompting, many LLMs can also proofread and edit content. LanguageTool is an open-source grammar checker supporting multiple languages, while Hemingway Editor is ideal for readability and sentence structure improvement. You can easily detect the content's complexity and adjust the level for a preferred audience.

Prompts:

- "Edit the following for structure, clarity, and conciseness: [PASTE TEXT]. Suggest improvements without changing meaning."
- "Check the following for grammar, punctuation, and sentence structure: [PASTE CONTENT]. Return corrected text with explanations for major changes."
- "Revise this to improve readability for C-suite executives. Use plain language, reduce jargon, and tighten sentences."

Language and Style

AI can adapt content style and language based on target audiences, whether formal and technical for B2B communications or conversational and engaging for customer-facing content. This flexibility aids marketing teams in optimizing messaging effectiveness across different platforms and international markets.

When editing content, remember to use guardrails whenever possible to control output and avoid hallucinations or unwanted additions. You might want to explicitly prompt AI to follow a specific tone and style. Where relevant, incorporate the prompt techniques discussed earlier, such as negative prompting to guide the model what it must avoid.

Prompt: "Reframe this [TEXT] for professional B2B communication to appeal directly to customers using benefit-infused language. Avoid being too salesy."

Plagiarism and Fact-Checking

AI-powered plagiarism detection tools safeguard original content creation by scanning vast databases to verify uniqueness, which is critical for maintaining brand integrity and avoiding legal risks. Additionally, AI fact-checkers provide automated verification of data points and statistics, which is invaluable for business reports, white papers, and thought leadership articles.

Plagiarism and fact-checking tools, such as Duplichecker, not only include reference links for quick citation generation but also come with an in-built paraphraser that provides real-time suggestions. Consider the following prompt examples:

- "For each claim in this document, provide source evidence (URL or citation), flag unverifiable claims, and suggest wording that accurately reflects the evidence."
- "Scan the text for similarity against web and academic databases. Return a report with matched sources and similarity scores."

AI Detection and Humanization

As AI-generated content becomes more prevalent, tools that detect AI-produced text and help humanize such content ensure authenticity and maintain trust with stakeholders. Organizations publishing work products or branded content must ensure their content reflects human expertise, not just algorithmic output. Stakeholders can distinguish between generative assistance and original thought and determine compliance with editorial or regulatory policies. Therefore, businesses can leverage AI detection and humanization solutions to balance efficiency with a human touch, critical for customer engagement and internal communications.

Some of the pioneers in AI detection and humanizing AI-generated content include Duplichecker, QuillBot, and ZeroGPT. Nonetheless, you must bear in mind that the accuracy of AI-detecting tools remains questionable, as they often include blank spaces and other irrelevant elements in their analysis. Therefore, you can use the tools for guidance but not to entirely pass off every flagged piece of content as AI-generated.

- **AI detection prompt:** "Assess this text for the likelihood of AI generation. Highlight sections with clear AI signatures and suggest revisions."
- **Humanizing output prompt:** "Take this AI-generated draft and rewrite it to make the voice distinctly human, keeping insights accurate and expressive."

It's worth noting that using AI to humanize AI-generated content still requires an actual human reviewer and overseer to ensure quality. AI tends to struggle with being concise and direct, which is why an AI-generated piece is likely to go in cycles and contain a bunch of sentences that say the same thing in different ways. A human reviewer can ensure that the message hits the right spot and resonates with the target audience.

Manuscript Formatting

Formatting large documents with consistent headings, references, lists, tables, and styles can engulf your productive time. AI tools can handle structural consistency and export-ready formats. For example, if you're a self-publishing author in charge of ensuring your manuscript meets Amazon KDP formatting guidelines, AI tools can be a huge benefit. Other notable platforms include Apple Books, Barnes & Noble, IngramSpark, Lulu, or any other print-on-demand services.

Alternatively, you might be a business professional wanting to effortlessly conform documents to organizational standards or publication requirements. AI can help format any document to meet the specified criteria. Document types with strict formatting requirements include policy papers with APA/Chicago citation compliance, technical manuals needing a standardized structure with a table of contents and cross-references, and investor memoranda where layout and hierarchy matter.

Grammarly add-ins can help with contextual grammar or style within a format, and ProWritingAid checks readability metrics and structure. Dedicated workflow tools, like Overleaf (for LaTeX) with AI extensions, Notion AI, or Copilot in Microsoft Word, are also effective with various output formats.

Here's a prompt example you can use with most LLMs and formatting tools: "Review this document for formatting consistency: heading levels, bulleted lists, and citation style [SPECIFY PREFERRED STYLE (APA, MLA, OR CHICAGO)]. Return a version ready for publishing."

THE AI-POWERED CONTENT CREATION PIPELINE

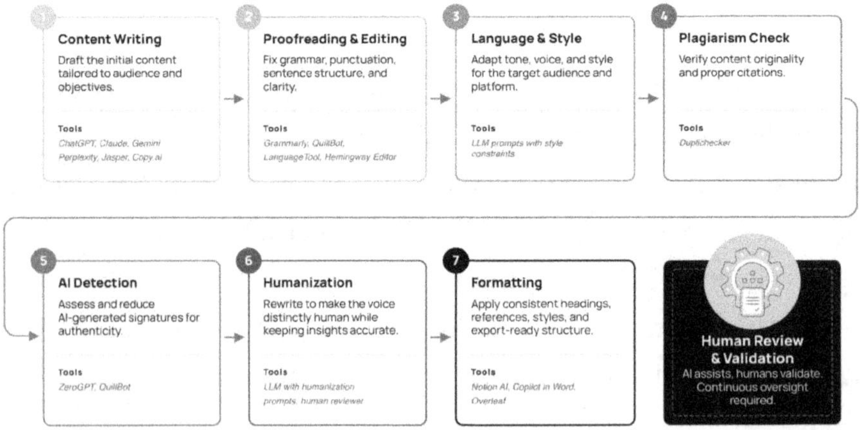

Image and Video Generation

Multimedia generation is another area where AI truly excels, enhancing creativity and productivity. The idea that you can create compelling images and engaging videos in minutes, without any prior graphic design skills, is mind-blowing, to say the least! If you've been looking to enhance your creativity and innovation through effective prompt engineering, you can now leverage image and video generation technologies to bring your ideas to life in unique and impactful ways. By crafting precise and imaginative prompts, you can guide AI tools to generate visuals and multimedia content that align closely with your business objectives, marketing strategies, or product designs.

Image Generation

Today's AI image generation tools combine aesthetic quality, prompt flexibility, style customization, and workflow integration. This enables your teams to create and scale visual assets without the heavy overhead of a designer. Anyone can visualize their task within minutes and present the draft without waiting for the design department to conceptualize it. That's an extra resource you can allocate to strategies, distribution, and further client reach and retention.

Some of the tools leading the image generation wave include Midjourney, OpenAI's DALL·E, Adobe Firefly, Canva AI, Gemini's Nano Banana from Google, and Stable Diffusion. ChatGPT has also rolled out a new image generation feature integrated within the LLM that enables you to see detailed prompts of predefined templates, which you can easily use to enhance your images. These tools vary in their artistic, high-quality styles, clean layouts, text-to-image precision, customization, and fine-tuning capabilities. You can choose your tool depending on the tasks at hand.

For example, you can opt for Midjourney's artistic styles for branding concepts, campaign visuals, and mood boards, and use DALL·E's text-to-image precision for product mock-ups, illustrations, and UI concepts. If you want quick social graphics or presentations, Canva AI is your go-to tool. Stable Diffusion is an open-source tool that offers extensive customization and is popular for iterative creative projects and fine-tuning prompts.

Irrespective of the model you choose, remember that feeding AI with enough details, clear instructions, and examples of the expected output can enhance your prompts to yield high-quality results. For example, you can upload branding guidelines or color palettes, or input any knowledge base for the model's reference to align its generation. Take a look at the following business examples where image generation tools can be impactful:

- A consulting firm preparing a client road map can use Midjourney to generate a visual metaphor set, which involves a series of stylized images representing stages of digital transformation (discovery→adoption→optimization). These visuals are then incorporated into the client deck, elevating audience comprehension and engagement.
- A hardware start-up can use DALL·E to create initial product concept renders based on descriptive prompts. These can be used in internal reviews and investor decks before full industrial design investment.
- A marketing team can use Canva AI to generate tailored visuals for multiple demographic segments, such as visuals with age-specific themes, and schedule variants for A/B performance testing.

Prompts:

- **Brand concept visualization:** "Create a series of five images that depict the journey of a customer adopting a tech platform: 1) Discovery, 2) Evaluation, 3) Onboarding, 4) Mastery, 5) Advocacy. The style should be clean, modern corporate illustrations with a consistent color palette."
- **Product mock-ups:** "Generate high-resolution concept images of a next-gen wearable device with a metallic finish and minimal UI displayed on screen, in contextual use (on a wrist, in an office, or outdoors). Ensure that the output has four unique design variants."
- **Campaign visual A/B sets:** "Produce two contrasting visuals for a sustainability campaign: Variation A: Earth tones and organic textures, and Variation B: Futuristic neon palette. Include simple typography and space for the headline."
- **Infographic elements:** "Design individual infographic elements for a report, including a pie chart icon, flow arrows, data nodes,

and team silhouettes. Style: flat design, brand color #002C71 and accent #F2A900." You can also specify these in simple language, such as navy blue and vivid orange, or choose any color you prefer. Canva AI already knows how color tones match with different accents and the specific combination codes; therefore, you don't have to know them, as your design teams do. However, being specific and using design jargon often ensures accuracy.

- **Product design conceptualization:** "Create a vibrant, futuristic cityscape at sunset featuring diverse professionals collaborating in a high-tech open office, with neon accents and a dynamic, optimistic atmosphere." This kind of prompt can help marketing teams visualize and pitch innovative urban tech concepts through compelling visuals.
- **Model an existing creative ad or visual:** "Analyze this visual [INSERT KNOWLEDGE BASE/FILE/URL, etc.], keep all branding elements unchanged, and generate 10 variations reflecting [PRODUCT] on a [BACKGROUND SETTING] with a vibrant, modern style. Target young urban professionals, and emphasize innovation through a cool color palette, diverse compositions, and layered imagery. Ensure the product remains the focal point, subtly altering background details to evoke energy and sophistication, while preserving logo placement and tagline visibility."

Video Generation

Traditional video production involves scripting, filming, editing, and postproduction. This process often takes hours or days, but AI consolidates all of it within minutes. With various AI tools now accessible, you can create engaging videos from simple text-to-video or image-to-video prompts. There has recently been a spike in behemoth companies, such as Coca-Cola, Cadbury, Nestlé, and Lexus, deploying AI in their ad campaigns.

Among these trailblazers, Spectrum Reach partnered with Waymark Cinematic and created 15,000 AI-powered ad campaigns, including one featuring Fun Spot America (Theme Parks). Fun Spot America's CEO said he was amazed at the speed with which AI created a cinematic-quality broadcast video and its ability to "bring an alligator to life," something that ensured they stood out from the competition (Winslow, 2025).

AI with human-in-the-loop creates exceptional collaboration. Inputting descriptive prompts with structure, including subject, details/action, setting/background, style, mood/palette, lighting/composition, and camera lens quality, can yield compelling visuals. Specify the main subject, appearance, environment, style (e.g., photorealistic, hyperrealistic, cinematic, or minimalistic), close-up, 4K, and mood (e.g., dark and dramatic, warm wood, or vibrant colors). Below are some of the top video generation tools and prompts:

- **Training video animation prompt:** "Produce a smooth 30-second animated video demonstrating a step-by-step guide on using a new SaaS platform dashboard, with clear UI highlights and engaging character animations."
- **Image-to-video generation prompt:** "Create a hyperrealistic visual of a confident businesswoman analyzing financial graphs on a transparent digital screen in a modern glass-walled office overlooking a city skyline at sunset. Style the image with a cinematic feel, warm golden tones, soft natural lighting highlighting her focused expression, captured with a high-quality 85 mm lens for sharp close-up detail and 4K resolution."
- You can use this prompt in a text-to-video AI tool or input the generated image in an image-to-video tool and describe what

should move. For example, describe how the subject uses hand gestures or blinks, or describe camera motion (close-up and zoom out). If you're not familiar with cinematography prompts, ChatGPT or any LLM can help you generate a detailed prompt and script that you can paste in an image-to-video AI tool like Hailuo, Invideo, or Artistly.

- **Invideo AI** and **Runway:** Both provide easy-to-use video editing and generation features, integrating AI-driven visual effects and animations. The text-to-video clips are perfect for short marketing videos and concept trailers.
- **HeyGen** and **Synthesia:** Specialize in AI-generated video content with customizable avatars and voiceovers, perfect for training videos and corporate communications. You can also use B-rolls for creative and attention-grabbing visuals.
- **Pika Labs:** Provides high-quality motion and prompt variability, perfect for visual storytelling and product demos.
- **Kling AI, Sora, Nano Banana, and Veo3:** These are versatile text-to-video and image-to-video generators that are integrated in popular AI tools such as Artlist, ChatGPT, and Gemini. Depending on your subscription plan, you can use these tools to generate short- or long-form content in hyperrealistic, cinematic, whimsical, or animation styles.

It's worth noting that image and video generation use a lot of processing power, which is why most tools come with limited token usage, depending on your plan. This necessitates being vigilant on how costly your experimentation becomes as you explore different models.

Key Takeaways

- AI serves as a powerful creative partner for ideation and brainstorming through techniques like disruptive thinking, challenging idea framing, diversified brainstorming, concept enhancement, and scenario exploration.
- Overcoming creative blocks becomes easier with AI, which can generate fresh perspectives, alternative approaches, and unexpected connections that break through mental stagnation.
- Structured problem-solving frameworks, including design thinking, SWOT analysis, Lean Six Sigma, PDCA cycles, Six Thinking Hats, and Ishikawa diagrams, can be prompted through AI to systematically analyze and solve complex challenges.
- AI accelerates content drafting and editing workflows, from initial writing and proofreading to style adjustments, plagiarism checks, AI detection humanization, and manuscript formatting.
- Image and video generation tools expand creative possibilities, but they require specific, detailed prompts with clear artistic direction to produce professional-quality visual content.

CHAPTER

6

LEVERAGING AI TO BOOST YOUR MARKETING AND SALES

Enriched with statistics from giant companies that prove the visible effectiveness of AI in boosting marketing and sales, this chapter is your North Star to growing your business by leveraging the technology. From conducting thorough market research to harnessing the power of social media marketing, search engine optimization (SEO), ads copywriting, and email marketing, AI makes client outreach and engagement through the entire buyer's journey until lead conversion blissful.

This chapter also includes prompt examples, the best tools for certain tasks, and case studies of successful companies already enjoying the benefits of AI integration. While the prompts are written simply to sum up each section, I recommend using the deep research or thinking mode feature when prompting AI for insightful and rich outputs. You can also refer to the prompt library in Chapter 8 and see how it incorporates the advanced techniques we discussed earlier to enrich simple prompts.

Market Research

High-performing marketing and sales activities are built on creativity and clarity about the customer, the market, value, pricing, and positioning. Historically, market research was slow, expensive, and quickly outdated. Today, AI has transformed market research into a living decision-support system that leaders can query continuously as markets shift. When prompted correctly, AI becomes your market analyst, customer psychologist, pricing strategist, and positioning adviser, all at once.

Target Audience Profiling

Most businesses still define audiences too broadly: for example, "SMBs," "millennials," and "enterprise clients." According to McKinsey &

Company reports, companies that use advanced customer analytics outperform peers by 126% in profit growth (Dobariya, 2025). The reason for this is that relevance drives results. AI enables multidimensional audience profiling, including demographics, psychographics, behavioral triggers, decision-making criteria, and media consumption patterns.

One of the interesting case studies on target audience profiling involves a popular streaming platform. Spotify uses AI-driven audience profiling to create hyperpersonalized playlists and campaigns. This deep customer understanding, which is far more than generic demographic targeting, has been a major driver of engagement and retention.

Prompt: "Act as a senior market research analyst specializing in [INDUSTRY]. Based on my business [BUSINESS NAME AND DESCRIPTION], current customer base [DESCRIBE], and core offer [PRODUCT/SERVICE], build three detailed target audience profiles that go beyond basic demographics. For each profile, include psychographics, emotional buying triggers, top three objections, decision-making process, preferred communication channels, and a day-in-the-life narrative showing when they'd seek my solution. Prioritize profiles by revenue potential, distinguish between decision-makers and influencers if B2B, and avoid generic labels like "millennials" or "SMBs." Format each as a structured persona card."

Technique applied: *Role priming + constraint layering + structured output.*

Defining Customer Pain Points

Customers don't always buy products on impulse, but they do buy relief from pain or movement toward desire. Companies that deeply understand customer pain points are significantly more likely to innovate successfully. AI helps extract pain points from reviews, support tickets, social conversations, sales call summaries, and industry discussions.

You can embed links or paste the knowledge base into the prompt for richer outputs.

Understanding your ideal customer's pain points and doing more analytical profiling work can serve as the basis for creating the personas discussed in the previous chapter, which are basically buckets of user archetypes that the profiling data can help to define. This allows marketing messages and sales conversations to mirror the customer's inner dialogue, which can dramatically increase conversion.

Prompt: "Act as a customer psychology researcher with expertise in [INDUSTRY]. My business category is [CATEGORY], targeting [PRIMARY AUDIENCE SEGMENT], competing with [TOP 2–3 COMPETITORS]. Using the data I've provided [REVIEWS/SUPPORT TICKETS/SURVEYS/SOCIAL MEDIA, paste or attach as a file], identify and rank my audience's top five pain points across emotional, functional, and financial dimensions. For each, include: the evidence or signal where this pain surfaces publicly, urgency level, and a one-sentence messaging hook that mirrors the customer's inner dialogue. Ground pain points in observable behavior, not assumptions. Present as a ranked table with columns: Pain Point | Type | Urgency | Evidence | Messaging Angle."

Technique applied: *Role priming + analytical decomposition + evidence-based constraints.*

Market Trend Identification

Markets rarely change overnight, but they often shift quietly before most business leaders notice. AI excels at pattern recognition across fragmented data, which can help you to spot emerging behaviors, declining demand signals, new category language, and adjacent opportunities. Historically, early trend recognition is one of the strongest predictors of long-term competitive advantage. Among trailblazers proving this point to be true, Netflix identified the shift toward on-demand, personalized consumption long before traditional broadcasters reacted. Their early trend recognition—powered by data—reshaped the entire entertainment industry.

Prompt: "Think like a world-class, forward-thinking trendsetter specializing in [INDUSTRY], and prepare me for a market shift by identifying emerging trends, technologies, and behavioral shifts in my market over the next three to five years."

Consumer Sentiment Analysis

Understanding how the market feels requires knowing how buying decisions are made. In most cases, they're not just rational decisions but rather emotional decisions justified logically. AI-driven sentiment analysis allows businesses to understand trust levels, frustrations, excitement, skepticism, and brand perception. In most cases, brands that align with consumer sentiment tend to outperform competitors in both loyalty and growth. AI can give you insight into how your specific market feels. This can guide you to frame your messaging, tone, and timing across marketing and sales channels in a manner that aligns.

Prompt: "Act as a consumer insights analyst specializing in brand perception research. For my brand [BRAND NAME] in the [CATEGORY] space, map the dominant sentiment themes consumers express across [GOOGLE REVIEWS/REDDIT/TWITTER/TRUSTPILOT/INDUSTRY FORUMS]. Identify the top three emotional drivers behind purchase decisions and top three objections or trust barriers. Compare my brand sentiment against [COMPETITOR 1] and [COMPETITOR 2] if publicly observable. Distinguish between category-level and brand-specific sentiment, flag where data may be limited, and present as a sentiment summary table with an objection map including suggested messaging responses."

Technique applied: *Role priming + comparative analysis + structured output.*

Estimating Market Size and Opportunity

Strategic growth requires understanding how big the opportunity actually is. AI can help estimate total addressable market (TAM), serviceable available market (SAM), and serviceable obtainable market (SOM). TAM means the maximum revenue opportunity available for the 100% market of a product or service based on total users. SAM refers to a realistic portion based on product offerings, target audience, and deliverables, while SOM means a narrowed market share that's realistically achievable within SAM. Understanding these metrics prevents overinvestment in small markets and underinvestment in large ones.

Prompt: "Act as a market sizing strategist with experience in [INDUSTRY] venture analysis. My business [BUSINESS NAME AND DESCRIPTION] offers [CORE OFFER] to [TARGET CUSTOMER SEGMENT] in [REGION/COUNTRY/GLOBAL], currently at [REVENUE OR "PRE-REVENUE"]. Estimate my market opportunity using both top-down and bottom-up approaches for TAM, SAM, and SOM within [TIME HORIZON]. For each tier, provide the calculation logic, assumptions, data sources or benchmarks, and confidence level (high/medium/low). State all assumptions explicitly so I can challenge them, use conservative estimates for SOM, and present as a tiered summary with a visual-ready breakdown."

Technique applied: *Role priming + assumption transparency + scenario analysis.*

Determining Market Share and Competitive Position

Similarly, you can determine market share to gain a competitive position. AI can analyze competitive presence, brand visibility, relative positioning, and share of voice. This provides strategic context for marketing spend and sales focus. You can start with the following prompt and refine as needed.

Prompt: "Act as a competitive intelligence analyst with deep expertise in [INDUSTRY]. My business is [BUSINESS NAME, CORE OFFER, POSITIONING]. My top competitors are [COMPETITOR 1, 2, 3—include URLs or descriptions]. My perceived strengths are [LIST] and weaknesses are [LIST]. Estimate relative market share for each competitor, analyze their positioning strategy and pricing approach, identify their strengths and exploitable weaknesses, and map where I'm defensibly strong vs. vulnerable. Present as a comparison table (Competitor | Est. Share | Positioning | Strengths | Weaknesses | Threat

Level) with three prioritized strategic moves. Base estimates on publicly observable signals and flag low-confidence items."

Technique applied: *Role priming + comparative framework + epistemic humility.*

Identifying Valuable Market Segments

Since not all customers are equal, profit concentration can be extreme in most industries, with a small subset of customers driving the majority of value. AI helps segment markets by profitability, willingness to pay, retention likelihood, and expansion potential. The following prompt can give you clarity and help you identify valuable market segments.

Prompt: "Act as a market segmentation strategist for [INDUSTRY] businesses. My business [BUSINESS NAME AND DESCRIPTION] currently serves [DESCRIBE YOUR CUSTOMER TYPES OR ATTACH DATA] with an average deal size of [AMOUNT OR RANGE], acquired primarily through [CHANNELS]. Segment my market into four to six groups based on revenue potential, growth trajectory, acquisition ease, retention likelihood, and lifetime value. For each segment, provide a name, value ranking (Tier 1/2/3), recommended acquisition approach, and one unique insight. Rank by overall strategic value (not just revenue), highlight any underserved "hidden gem" segments, and present as a prioritized table with recommended resource allocation."

Technique applied: *Role priming + multi-criteria segmentation + strategic prioritization.*

Forecasting Market Growth

To avoid guesswork, important decisions must be based on market growth forecasts. AI can synthesize historical data, trends, and external signals to produce scenario-based forecasts. It allows leaders to plan capacity, marketing investment, and hiring with confidence.

Prompt: "Act as a market forecasting analyst specializing in [INDUSTRY] within [REGION]. The current market size is approximately [IF KNOWN, OR "UNKNOWN"], with key growth drivers including [LIST 2–3] and key headwinds including [LIST 2–3]. Provide a three-scenario growth forecast over [TIME HORIZON]: conservative (headwinds persist, slow adoption), moderate (current trajectory, gradual improvement), and aggressive (tailwinds accelerate, barriers fall). For each scenario, include the estimated annual growth rate, key assumptions, and implications for my business (hiring, investment, positioning). State assumptions transparently, cite benchmarks used, and present as a scenario comparison table with a recommended planning scenario."

Technique applied: *Role priming + scenario analysis + assumption transparency.*

Pricing Strategy Research

Both Bain & Company and *Harvard Business Review* report that companies that base pricing on perceived value rather than production cost outperform competitors in profitability (Gallo, 2014; Reichheld, 2001). The goal is to ensure that you understand how much customers value your service based on what they think about it. Since customers mostly buy with emotions, the value they associate with your product or service is often less about the cost of producing it and more about how much they're willing to pay for it.

Most luxury brands capitalize on this customer-focused pricing strategy. You can charge a premium price if you justify it with the value of your service. AI can help identify differentiators that customers value, emotional benefits worth paying for, and messaging that supports premium positioning. It can also help you analyze competitor pricing, price sensitivity, value drivers, and customers' willingness to pay.

Apple is a common case study of a company that excels at value perception and premium pricing. It consistently commands premium pricing through perceived value, not just through features alone. From design to ecosystem and brand story, Apple's pricing strategy is inseparable from market research and messaging discipline.

Prompts: "Act as a pricing strategist with expertise in value-based pricing for [INDUSTRY]. My offer is [PRODUCT/SERVICE] currently priced at [PRICE OR "NOT YET SET"] with [COST STRUCTURE IF KNOWN], targeting [CUSTOMER SEGMENT]. My top competitors charge [COMPETITOR 1: $X, COMPETITOR 2: $Y]. Analyze the pricing landscape (premium, mid-tier, budget), identify which elements of my offering support premium positioning, and recommend an optimal pricing strategy with rationale. Present your analysis as: a market pricing map (Competitor | Price | Positioning | Justification), my recommended price with logic, and three messaging angles that reinforce the price-value relationship. Ground recommendations in customer willingness to pay, address the most likely price objection, and flag assumptions where data is limited."

Technique applied: *Role priming + competitive benchmarking + constraint layering.*

Market Messaging Tests Before Full Launch

Testing your market messaging before full launch is crucial. AI allows rapid message testing without large budgets. You can test headlines, value propositions, objection handling, and emotional resonance.

Prompt: "Act as a positioning and messaging strategist specializing in pre-launch validation. I'm launching [PRODUCT/SERVICE] for [PRIMARY AUDIENCE SEGMENT]. My current value proposition is [YOUR BEST VERSION] and my competitors position themselves as [DESCRIBE]. Generate five messaging variations using different angles: outcome-driven, pain-agitation, curiosity-based, social proof, and authority/credibility. For each, explain the psychological mechanism it leverages and score it on clarity, emotional resonance, and differentiation (1–10 each). Recommend the top two for A/B testing with rationale. Each variation must be genuinely distinct in approach, not just rewording, and avoid generic marketing language like "innovative" or "world-class." Score it honestly. At least one variation should score below 5 on at least one criterion to ensure your scoring actually discriminates between options. Present as a comparison table with scores."

Technique applied: *Role priming + multi-angle generation + self-evaluation scoring.*

Finding and Refining a Strong Value Proposition

All of the sections above are attempts to help you reach a strong value proposition. The primary reason for conducting thorough market research is to position yourself, your products, or your services in a manner that seems valuable to the customer. You want to justify why a customer must choose you over similar businesses. A strong value proposition answers three questions clearly: Who is this for? What problem does it solve? Why is it better or different? AI helps you to articulate this with precision.

Prompt: "Act as a positioning strategist specializing in value proposition development for [INDUSTRY]. My business [BUSINESS NAME AND WHAT YOU DO] serves [MOST VALUABLE SEGMENT], whose top priority is [THEIR #1 PAIN POINT]. My core differentiator is [WHAT MAKES YOU DIFFERENT], and my current value proposition is [PASTE IT OR "NONE YET"]. Evaluate it against: Who is this for? What problem does it solve? Why is it better? Then craft three variations—outcome-driven, pain-driven, and differentiation-driven—each in two sentences maximum. Recommend the strongest version and where to deploy it (homepage, pitch deck, email header, ad copy). Avoid vague language like "best-in-class" and test each against: "Could a competitor say this?" If yes, it's not differentiated enough."

Technique applied: *Role priming + multi-angle generation + competitive differentiation test.*

Social Media Marketing

Contrary to common belief, social media isn't just about posting more content but about earning attention, building trust, and guiding buying decisions over time. According to Edelman's 2019–2025 *Trust Barometer* reports, up to 81% of buyers say trust in a brand strongly influences their purchasing decisions (Holliday, 2025). Social media is now one of the primary arenas where that trust is formed or lost. AI enables leaders and businesses to move from reactive posting to intentional, data-driven social strategy.

Strategic Role of Social Media in Marketing and Sales

High-performing companies use social media to shape market perception, educate before selling, warm up leads before sales conversations, and reinforce brand authority. It isn't surprising that McKinsey research shows that brands with strong digital engagement outperform peers in revenue growth by up to 20% (Bough et al., 2023). AI can help you to orchestrate this strategically. LinkedIn Sales Navigator also reveals that 78% of social sellers outperform peers who don't use social media strategically (Castro, 2024; The Daily Sales, 2024; LinkedIn, n.d.).

AI helps sales teams to warm up prospects, personalize outreach, and reference shared content narratives. Tools like Pomelli, Board Ad, and Bacon can also extract your website content and brand elements and integrate them into your social media posts for authoritative brand consistency.

Audience and Platform Alignment

Different platforms serve different buying psychologies. LinkedIn is ideal for building authority, thought leadership, B2B trust, and long-cycle sales. X (formerly Twitter) works best for thought leadership, visibility, and conversations. Instagram is perfect for brand perception, lifestyle, and emotional appeal. TikTok is your go-to platform for discovery, virality, and narrative storytelling. YouTube excels at long-form education and conversion. AI helps match audience intent to platform behavior. It can also simplify content repurposing across multiple platforms.

Prompt: "Act as a social media strategist specializing in platform selection for [INDUSTRY] businesses. I'm a [B2B/B2C/D2C] business targeting [PRIMARY SEGMENT—age, role, interests], with a goal of

[BRAND AWARENESS / LEAD GENERATION / DIRECT SALES / COMMUNITY BUILDING]. I'm currently on [PLATFORMS] and can realistically produce [AMOUNT] content per week. Rank the top three platforms by strategic fit, explaining why each fits, what content format works best, and expected ROI timeline. Identify one platform to deprioritize with rationale. Suggest a content repurposing strategy across the recommended platforms. Factor in my content capacity—don't recommend five platforms if I can only produce for two."

Technique applied: *Role priming + capacity-aware planning + strategic prioritization.*

Content Creation and Strategy

Successful companies often publish educational and value-driven content, which studies reveal generates three times more leads (Huang, 2024). AI can help you design content pillars, such as educational insights, market commentary, case studies, outcomes, behind-the-scenes credibility signals, and customer success narratives.

Prompt: "Act as a content strategist who builds social media systems for [INDUSTRY] brands. My brand positioning is [YOUR POSITIONING STATEMENT], targeting [PRIMARY SEGMENT], with a sales goal of [LEADS/BOOKINGS/PURCHASES/AWARENESS]. My brand voice is [DESCRIBE TONE], and I primarily publish on [PLATFORMS]. Define four to six content pillars, each with a clear strategic purpose (educate, build trust, drive action, humanize). For each pillar, provide a description, three example post ideas adapted to my platform's format, and the sales goal it supports. Map the pillars to a weekly posting rhythm and include one "wild card" pillar for trending content. Every pillar must connect to brand building or revenue and no filler."

Technique applied: *Role priming + system design + output formatting.*

AI also enables audience-specific messaging, adaptive tone and framing, and persona-based content variations. This can help you personalize your content in a way that resonates with specific audiences.

Prompt: "Act as a social media messaging specialist for [INDUSTRY]. Here is my original message: [PASTE MESSAGE]. Rewrite it for three different audience segments: [SEGMENT 1], [SEGMENT 2], and [SEGMENT 3]. For each version, adjust the tone, emphasis, pain points addressed, and CTA to match what that segment cares about most. Explain the key shift you made for each and why it resonates differently. Keep all versions platform-appropriate for [PLATFORM] and maintain brand consistency across all three."

Technique applied: *Role priming + audience segmentation + adaptive messaging.*

AI supports post-ideation, caption writing, video scripts, carousel narratives, and repurposing long-form content into short-form assets. For example, serial entrepreneur, renowned author, and internet mentor Gary Vaynerchuk (commonly known as GaryVee) has a dedicated team that repurposes his long-form content into dozens of platform-specific assets. You can adopt his approach using AI tools such as Opus Clip, Headliner, Descript, Riverside, and Quso.ai. Some of these platforms already auto-schedule your posts across various social media platforms.

Prompt: "Act as an elite social media manager and content strategist for [INDUSTRY]. Here is my long-form content: [PASTE OR LINK ARTICLE/VIDEO/PODCAST]. Repurpose it into 10 platform-specific posts optimized for engagement across [PLATFORMS]. Include a mix of formats: text posts, carousel concepts, quote graphics, short-form video scripts, and thread or story breakdowns. For each post, specify the platform, format, hook, and CTA. Ensure each can stand alone without requiring the audience to read the original. Sequence them for a two-week posting schedule."

Technique applied: *Role priming + multi-format repurposing + scheduling.*

Engagement, Community, and Trust Signals

Social algorithms reward interaction over mere broadcasting. AI can suggest conversation prompts, draft thoughtful responses, identify engagement opportunities, and analyze comment sentiment. With highly efficient tools like GoHighLevel and ManyChat, you can even automate social media comments and conversations to increase your response rate. For instance, you can embed keywords within your content that prompt your audience to take action. AI can recognize these keyword-triggered responses, and your autoresponder then takes care of the comments or follows up on direct messages to keep your community engaged.

Prompts: "Act as a community engagement strategist for [PLATFORM] specializing in trust-driven audiences. I currently have approximately [FOLLOWER COUNT] followers with a [LOW/MEDIUM/HIGH] engagement rate. My best-performing content is [DESCRIBE], and my biggest challenge is [LOW COMMENTS / NO SHARES / STALLED GROWTH / etc.]. Diagnose the top three reasons my engagement may be underperforming, recommend five specific tactics to increase meaningful interactions (comments, saves, shares, DMs—not vanity metrics), and suggest a trust-building content sequence of three to five posts. Also identify one engagement pattern I should stop. Present tactics as a prioritized action list with expected impact level, executable within my current content capacity."

Technique applied: *Role priming + diagnostic analysis + actionable prioritization.*

Social Media Content Calendar

In addition to interaction, social media algorithms also reward consistency. It's crucial to keep your audience engaged with fresh (or repurposed) content, either through social media posts, reels, or stories. AI can help you plan your posting schedule, so you never run out of things to say. You can prompt AI to create a social media content calendar for a week, a month, or longer. Tools like Hootsuite, SocialBee (which integrates with Canva and Unsplash), Sprout Social, Later, and Buffer can also be helpful if you want to schedule and automate your posts to publish at the optimal times for audience engagement.

SEO Content

While social media builds awareness, SEO elevates and captures existing demand. When people search for your products or services, they reveal their intent to buy, which SEO helps convert into sales. According to HubSpot, over 90% of online experiences begin with a search engine (Ionita, 2025).

SEO remains one of the highest-ROI marketing channels that support long-term demand generation, lower customer acquisition cost, sales enablement, and brand authority. High-performing companies map SEO content directly to awareness, consideration, and decision stages. Subsequently, AI supports funnel mapping, content gap identification, and lead capture optimization.

Keyword and Search Intent Research

AI can help you classify keywords by intent, from informational to commercial, transactional, and navigational. It can analyze a user's query to reflect whether they're merely searching for information, looking to complete a purchase, or trying to get to a specific site. You can then use this information to align with your website's purpose so that it ranks high on search engines, capturing clients searching for the solution you provide.

Prompt: "Act as an SEO strategist specializing in search intent mapping for [INDUSTRY]. My business [BUSINESS NAME] offers [TOP 3–5 PRODUCTS/SERVICES] to [TARGET AUDIENCE] with a [LOCAL/NATIONAL/GLOBAL] focus and currently [LOW/MEDIUM/HIGH] organic traffic. Identify 15–20 high-priority keywords, classify each by intent (informational, commercial, transactional, navigational), group them into three to four topic clusters, and recommend a priority order based on search volume potential, competition difficulty, and sales funnel alignment. Present as a keyword table (Keyword | Intent | Cluster | Funnel Stage | Priority) with three quick-win content opportunities. Prioritize keywords where I can realistically rank within [6/12] months and flag any cannibalization risks."

Technique applied: *Role priming + funnel mapping + strategic prioritization.*

Structured Content and Topic Clusters

AI also helps build pillar content, supporting cluster articles and internal linking strategies. HubSpot's growth was fueled by topic clusters and educational content that dominated search intent, long before its competitors caught up.

Prompt: "Act as an SEO content strategist specializing in topical authority building for [INDUSTRY]. My business [BUSINESS NAME] offers [CORE PRODUCTS/SERVICES], and my site currently ranks for [FEW/SOME/MANY] keywords in [CATEGORY]. Create a content cluster strategy with one pillar page and six to eight supporting cluster articles that position my site as an authority. For each piece, specify the target keyword, search intent, content format, and how it links back to the pillar. Prioritize topics where I can realistically compete, map each article to a funnel stage, and present as a cluster map with a recommended publishing sequence."

Technique applied: *Role priming + topical authority framework + funnel mapping.*

Content Depth and Relevance

Both Semrush and Ahrefs indicate that long-form, in-depth content significantly outperforms shallow articles in rankings and engagement. AI assists with structured outlines, search-aligned headlines, content depth optimization, and readability improvements.

Prompt: "Act as a senior SEO content strategist for [INDUSTRY]. Create a comprehensive outline for an article targeting the keyword [INSERT KEYWORD] for my site [WEBSITE/BUSINESS], which targets [AUDIENCE]. Include the primary and secondary user intent behind this keyword, a compelling headline with H2 and H3 subheadings, recommended word count, key subtopics for depth, internal linking opportunities to [EXISTING CONTENT IF ANY], and a suggested meta title and description. Address what searchers actually want to know, not just what's keyword-dense. Flag content gaps competitors are missing that I can capitalize on."

Technique applied: *Role priming + intent analysis + competitive gap identification.*

Outdated articles lose ranking over time. AI can identify declining pages, suggest updates, refresh examples and data, and maintain relevance.

Prompt: "Act as an SEO audit specialist for [INDUSTRY] websites. Analyze my existing content [PASTE URLs, TITLES, OR CONTENT LIST] and identify which pieces are losing search rankings. For each declining piece, diagnose the likely cause (outdated data, thin content, intent shift, new competition) and recommend specific updates: refreshed statistics, expanded sections, improved headers, updated examples, or restructured format. Prioritize by recovery potential (high/medium/low) and estimated effort. Present as an audit table: Article | Current Status | Decline Cause | Recommended Updates | Priority | Effort."

Technique applied: *Role priming + diagnostic audit + prioritized action plan.*

On-Page Optimization and Conversion Alignment

AI helps optimize meta titles and descriptions, headline hierarchy, internal links, and CTAs aligned with the buyer stage.

Prompt: "Act as an on-page SEO and conversion rate optimizer for [INDUSTRY]. Take this article [PASTE OR DESCRIBE CONTENT] targeting the keyword [KEYWORD] and optimize it for both search rankings and reader conversion. Improve the headline hierarchy (H1, H2, H3) for clarity and keyword relevance, write a compelling meta title and description, suggest internal links to [RELATED PAGES], and align CTAs with the reader's likely buyer stage. Ensure the optimization improves discoverability without sacrificing readability or sounding keyword-stuffed."

Technique applied: *Role priming + dual-objective optimization (SEO + conversion).*

Ads Copywriting

Sometimes, advertising fails because the messaging lacks clarity, relevance, and conviction, not because businesses lack visibility. To see recall and conversion, your ads must communicate the value of the product rather than the specifications. Copywriting involves structured persuasion, which is why copywriters charge premium amounts.

While collaborating with a human copywriter might be your best option if you don't know much about using words to sell, AI gives you leverage to turn plain, non-converting text into highly converting copy. AI allows you to systematize persuasion at scale, testing, refining, and optimizing copy across channels without losing strategic intent. You can integrate persona-driven techniques, such as prompting AI to embody the role of a world-class copywriter addressing a specific audience, to improve output.

Copywriting Headlines

Your headline determines whether anything else gets read. Your headline must be well-formatted and crafted to capture immediate attention because that's where most people decide if they want to interact with your ad or not. Effective headlines do one of three things: promise a clear outcome, address a painful problem, or spark curiosity grounded in relevance.

For example, Google's highest-performing ads consistently emphasize outcomes, not features. "Get more customers" beats "Advanced analytics tools."

Prompt: "Act as a world-class copywriter specializing in [INDUSTRY]. My offer is [PRODUCT/SERVICE] for [TARGET AUDIENCE] at [PRICE POINT]. The core benefit is [PRIMARY OUTCOME]. Generate 15 headline variations using three frameworks: five benefit-driven, five curiosity-based, and five problem–solution. Rank all 15 by clarity and conversion potential, and explain why your top three would stop a scrolling buyer. Avoid vague or hype-driven language — every headline must be specific enough that a reader immediately knows what's being offered and why it matters. Match tone to [BRAND VOICE]."

Technique applied: *Role priming + multi-framework generation + self-evaluation ranking.*

Website and Landing Page Copy

According to Stanford Web Credibility Research, 75% of users judge a company's credibility based on website copy and clarity (Drain, 2025). AI helps structure website and landing page copy around immediate value clarity, objection handling, trust signals, and logical flow. Additionally, focused landing pages can increase conversion rates by over 65% (Akolo,

2023). AI can help you design clear above-the-fold messaging, benefit-driven sections, risk reversal, proof and validation, and CTA alignment.

Prompts: "Act as a conversion-focused website copywriter specializing in [INDUSTRY]. My business [BUSINESS NAME] serves [TARGET AUDIENCE] with [CORE OFFER]. Here is my current website copy: [PASTE OR DESCRIBE]. Rewrite it to clearly communicate value within the first five seconds, address the top three objections my audience has [LIST IF KNOWN], and guide users toward [PRIMARY CONVERSION ACTION]. Structure with clear above-the-fold messaging, benefit-driven sections, trust signals (testimonials, credentials, guarantees), and a logical flow from problem to solution to action. Keep the tone [BRAND VOICE] and ensure clarity on mobile screens."

Technique applied: *Role priming + conversion architecture + objection handling.*

Perfect CTAs

Effective CTAs match the buyer's readiness, reduce perceived risk, and emphasize value, not effort. For example, "Get the free guide," "See how it works," and "Start improving results today" are CTA variations that indicate low friction, pique intrigue, and are outcome-driven, respectively.

Prompt: "Act as a conversion copywriter specializing in funnel-stage CTA optimization. My offer is [PRODUCT/SERVICE] for [PRIMARY AUDIENCE], placed on [LANDING PAGE / EMAIL / AD / SOCIAL POST]. My current CTA is [WHAT YOU'RE USING NOW]. Generate three CTA variations for each funnel stage: awareness (low-commitment, curiosity-driven), consideration (value-reinforcing, trust-building), and decision (urgency-driven, risk-reducing). For each, explain the psychological trigger it activates and when to use it. Keep all CTAs under eight words, avoid generic phrases like "Learn more" or "Click here," match tone to [BRAND VOICE], and present as a funnel-stage table."

Technique applied: *Role priming + funnel-stage mapping + psychological anchoring.*

Product Description

It's common for customers to consistently overvalue emotional benefits when making decisions, even in B2B contexts. A good product description highlights the benefits over features. Features explain a product, while benefits persuade action because they focus on what the customer gets from using the product. AI helps transform technical features into customer outcomes, functional value into emotional reassurance, and capabilities into use cases.

Prompt: "Act as a conversion-focused product copywriter for [INDUSTRY]. My product is [PRODUCT NAME] at [PRICE], targeting [BUYER PERSONA]. Here is the current description: [PASTE EXISTING DESCRIPTION]. My key competitor describes their product as [DESCRIBE]. Rewrite this description to lead with the primary outcome the buyer cares about, translate each feature into a benefit with a real-world use case, include one emotional reassurance statement, and end with a natural CTA transition. Keep under [WORD COUNT] words, write for [SOPHISTICATION LEVEL: general consumer / technical buyer / executive], and avoid superlatives or unsubstantiated claims. Format with a benefit-driven headline, two to three short paragraphs, and a closing CTA line."

Technique applied: *Role priming + benefit reframing + audience-aware constraints.*

Ad Copy

Each ad platform has its own psychology: Google Ads is intent-driven and problem-aware, Meta Ads is interruption-based and emotion-driven, and LinkedIn Ads is authority-driven and trust-based. AI helps tailor copy to platform norms, user mindset, and funnel stage. According to Meta, ads aligned with platform-native language significantly outperform generic repurposed copy (Cintra, 2025).

Prompt: "Act as a performance marketing copywriter experienced across Google, LinkedIn, and Meta ad platforms. My offer is [PRODUCT/SERVICE] for [TARGET AUDIENCE] at [PRICE POINT]. Write ad copy variations for each platform, adapting tone and framing to match platform psychology: Google (intent-driven, problem-aware), Meta (interruption-based, emotion-driven), and LinkedIn (authority-driven, trust-based). For each platform, provide two variations with different hooks, including the headline, body copy, and CTA. Explain why each variation works for its platform's user mindset. Keep within each platform's character limits."

Technique applied: *Role priming + platform-native psychology + multi-variant generation.*

Email Marketing

Email remains one of the highest-ROI channels. According to recent studies, email marketing delivers an average of $36–45 for every $1 spent, resulting in 3,600–4,500% ROI (Ellis & Evans, 2025). AI enables subject-line testing, personalization at scale, behavioral follow-ups, and sales-enablement sequences. You can send a series of emails that enrich your thought leadership and create trust on a topic related to your product and service while building and nurturing an audience you can profit from later.

Morning Brew makes 90% of its revenue from its email marketing strategy; it did this by creating a shared revenue model that rewards its loyal audience for sharing its newsletter (Bogore, 2023). It also helps that its content is entertaining, engaging, and educational, making it a no-brainer to circulate.

Prompt: "Act as an email marketing strategist specializing in lead nurturing for [INDUSTRY]. My business [BUSINESS NAME] offers [CORE OFFER] to [TARGET AUDIENCE]. Create a five-to-seven email sequence that nurtures leads from awareness to decision. For each email, include the strategic purpose, subject line, key message, one objection it addresses, a trust-building element, and the CTA. Map the sequence to the buyer's journey—early emails educate and build trust, middle emails reinforce value and handle objections, final emails create urgency and drive conversion. Keep the tone [BRAND VOICE] and ensure each email can stand alone if opened out of sequence."

Technique applied: *Role priming + buyer journey mapping + objection sequencing.*

Key Takeaways

- Comprehensive market research including target audience profiling, pain point analysis, trend identification, sentiment analysis, market sizing, and pricing strategy can be dramatically accelerated using AI-driven prompts.
- Social media marketing effectiveness depends on strategic platform alignment, consistent content creation, community engagement, and data-driven content calendars, all of which AI can help plan and execute.
- SEO content strategy benefits from AI assistance in keyword research, topic clustering, content depth optimization, and on-page optimization to drive organic traffic and conversions.
- High-converting ad copy from headlines and landing pages to CTAs, product descriptions, and email marketing campaigns, can be rapidly drafted and tested using targeted AI prompts.
- The most effective marketing and sales AI usage combines well-crafted prompts with human strategic oversight, ensuring that AI-generated content aligns with brand voice, audience needs, and business objectives.

CHAPTER

7

HOW TO GROW YOUR CAREER AND BUSINESS

For most of the 20th century, success followed a predictable formula: Choose a profession, climb the ladder, accumulate experience, and eventually reap the rewards. That linear career model is now collapsing, and today, professionals face a different reality. Roles evolve faster than job titles, and skills expire in years, sometimes months. Entire industries are reshaped by software, and leadership is no longer defined by how much you know but by how effectively you think, decide, and adapt. This is where AI changes the equation.

If you use AI effectively, it becomes more powerful than just a productivity tool. It can be a career architect that helps you design, test, and refine your professional path, a personal strategist that strengthens your brand, skills, and positioning, and a business cofounder that helps you research, plan, launch, and scale ventures with unprecedented speed. This chapter explores how to grow and accelerate your career and how to create, improve, and scale a business using AI.

Whether you plan to climb within an organization, reinvent yourself professionally, or build something entirely new, the principles remain the same: Set clear goals, use intelligent prompts, and execute strategically. You can incorporate advanced prompt techniques from earlier chapters to enrich the prompts or edit each prompt as shown in the library in the next chapter.

Career Planning Path

Clarifying Your Career Goals

Contrary to the common belief that some professionals fail because of a lack of talent, many people often fail because their goals are vague. "I want to grow." "I want a better role." "I want more impact." We've already established that AI becomes powerful once you move from vague ambition to a specific direction. For example, "Act as a senior career strategist. Help me clarify my ideal career direction over the next three to five years based on my current role, interests, income goals, lifestyle preferences, and long-term leadership aspirations."

AI can help you map multiple career scenarios (corporate, independent, and hybrid), stress-test each path for risk, growth, and sustainability, and identify hidden career adjacencies you may never have considered before. This is about designing optional paths and staying in control rather than worrying about choosing one perfect path.

Evaluating Your Current Skills

Career stagnation often comes from an outdated self-assessment. You may be strong in skills that no longer matter and weak in skills the market increasingly rewards. This is where you can leverage AI's structured analysis.

Prompt: "Act as a senior career strategist specializing in leadership development in [INDUSTRY]. My current role is [JOB TITLE] with [YEARS] of experience. My core skills are [LIST TOP 5–7], and I'm targeting [TARGET ROLE]. Evaluate my skills against the expectations of that role, categorizing each as: competitive strength, adequate, gap, or at risk of obsolescence. Identify the top three gaps that would most accelerate my progression and recommend one "hidden advantage" skill most professionals overlook. Present as a skills assessment table (Skill | Current Level | Target Expectation | Status | Priority Action) with development priorities. Factor in AI's impact on which skills are gaining or losing value."

***Technique applied**: Role priming + gap analysis + market-informed constraints.*

Understanding Skill Demand and Market Signals

As we saw in Chapter 4, one of AI's greatest advantages is its ability to synthesize large patterns. Rather than guessing which skills will matter, you can ask AI to analyze hiring trends, role evolution, cross-industry demand, and future-facing capabilities. This allows you to invest your learning time where it produces maximum return.

Prompt: "Act as a workforce trends analyst specializing in [INDUSTRY] career evolution. I'm a [JUNIOR/MID/SENIOR/EXECUTIVE]-level professional in [FIELD] based in [REGION], currently investing in [SKILLS LIST]. Identify the top five skills gaining demand over the next three to five years and two to three skills at risk of declining. For each high-demand skill, explain why it's rising, how to develop it, and estimated time to proficiency. Flag cross-industry skills that would give me a competitive edge. Base predictions on observable hiring trends, distinguish between "nice to have" and "career-defining," and present as a trend map with urgency ratings (invest now / watch / deprioritize)."

Technique applied: *Role priming + trend analysis + urgency-based prioritization.*

Creating a Personalized Learning Path

Once your skill gaps are clear, AI can help you design a step-by-step learning road map, prioritize skill acquisition, and suggest projects for real-world application.

Prompt: "Act as a leadership development coach who builds career acceleration plans. I'm currently a [JOB TITLE] targeting [DESIRED POSITION] within 12 months, with [HOURS] hours per week available for learning. I prefer [COURSES/BOOKS/PROJECTS/MENTORSHIP/CERTIFICATIONS] and my top three skill gaps are [LIST]. Create a quarterly road map: Q1 for foundation building, Q2 for applied practice, Q3 for visibility and positioning, Q4 for transition readiness. For each quarter, provide two to three learning objectives, specific resources or actions, a milestone deliverable that proves progress, and time allocation. Respect my weekly learning budget, balance technical, strategic, and AI skills, and include at least one "show your work" deliverable per quarter."

Technique applied: *Role priming + phased planning + capacity-aware constraints.*

Building a Personal Brand With AI Support

Today, your career is inseparable from your professional narrative, and AI can help you to balance that uniformity. It can help you clarify your professional identity, articulate your value clearly, and align your experience with future goals. Some of the key brand elements AI can help you shape include personal positioning statements, core expertise themes, thought leadership angles, and online presence consistency.

Prompt: "Act as a personal branding strategist for senior professionals in [INDUSTRY]. I'm currently [JOB TITLE AT COMPANY] with expertise in [TOP 3 STRENGTHS], aspiring to [WHERE YOU WANT TO BE IN 3–5 YEARS]. My brand needs to resonate with [RECRUITERS/CLIENTS/INDUSTRY PEERS/ALL] primarily on [LINKEDIN/PERSONAL SITE/SPEAKING]. Craft a professional brand statement (two to three sentences) that communicates my unique value, define three to four core brand themes to reinforce consistently, suggest a 30-day brand-building action plan, and write a LinkedIn headline and summary that align. Avoid buzzwords like "thought leader" or "passionate", ground the brand in outcomes and expertise, not self-description."

Technique applied: *Role priming + multi-output generation + anti-cliché constraints.*

Creating a Powerful Resume and Portfolio

While most resumes list history, strategic ones tell a trajectory story. AI can help you translate experience into outcomes, quantify impact, align language with executive expectations, and tirelessly customize your resume for different roles. It's often expected that leaders' portfolios will showcase strategic decisions, case studies, thought processes, and business impact. AI can frame that with precision.

Prompt: "Act as a senior executive resume strategist. Here is my current resume: [PASTE OR ATTACH]. I'm targeting [SPECIFIC JOB TITLE AND LEVEL] in [INDUSTRY], and my top three achievements are [LIST]. Rewrite each bullet point to lead with strategic impact instead of task description, quantify results wherever possible (revenue, %, time saved, team size), and highlight AI literacy and leadership influence. Ensure the resume tells a career progression story. Use action verbs that signal leadership ("orchestrated," "architected," "pioneered"), not "assisted" or "helped." Align language with senior-level expectations and format as ready-to-use bullet points grouped by role."

Technique applied: *Role priming + outcome-driven rewriting + constraint layering.*

You can also ask it to include verifiable case studies or hypothetical scenarios that you can use to practice for your interview, so that you leave a lasting impact that positions you as an ideal candidate for any leadership role.

Preparing for Interviews

Interviews are performance environments, and for leadership roles, the stakes are even higher. AI can prepare you through simulated executive-level interviews, behavioral questioning, case-based scenarios, and objection handling. You can leverage AI to present yourself as a sought-after candidate and beat any interview anxiety.

Prompt: "Act as a senior executive interviewer and leadership assessor for [INDUSTRY]. I'm preparing for a [BEHAVIORAL/CASE-BASED/PANEL/CONVERSATIONAL] interview for [JOB TITLE AND COMPANY TYPE]. My biggest strength is [STRENGTH] and my area of concern is [VULNERABILITY]. Ask me five challenging executive-level questions mixing behavioral, strategic, and situational formats. After each response, evaluate on clarity, leadership presence, strategic depth, and specificity. Provide constructive feedback with a rewritten "model answer" for weak responses, and ask follow-ups that probe vague answers. Be constructively critical, don't accept surface-level answers. End with an overall assessment and three specific areas to improve before the real interview. Begin by asking me the first question only, then wait for my response and evaluate it before moving to the next."

Technique applied: *Role priming + interactive simulation + evaluative feedback.*

Exploring Growth Opportunities and Overcoming Career Barriers

AI is especially useful when you feel stuck. It can help you to identify invisible bottlenecks, reframe setbacks, explore lateral or unconventional moves, and design risk-managed transitions. Career security increasingly comes from value creation, not job title. If you're seeking growth beyond employment, there's no better time to carve your path than today. AI dramatically lowers the barrier to entrepreneurship, but only if you seize the opportunity and think strategically.

Prompt: "Imagine you're a career analyst helping a mid-level manager who feels stagnant in their current role with limited promotion opportunities. Analyze their attached existing skills and market trends to identify new growth areas [PASTE OR UPLOAD RESUME]. Explore unconventional career paths such as freelance consulting or starting a side business related to their expertise. Develop a strategic plan for a risk-managed transition that leverages AI for market research, networking, and skill development to create value beyond their current job title."

Creating a New Business

From Idea to Opportunity

Most business ideas fail because they're built around passion rather than market reality. To build a profitable business that leverages your passion, you must allow yourself to approach the idea through the lens of a businessperson. AI excels at early-stage validation to ensure that you're focusing on something economically viable. It can help you refine ideas into viable offers, identify underserved niches, and spot strategic differentiation early. You can even ask it to reframe your existing idea into a profit-making machine by giving you the exact steps from idea to business launch and articulating how you'll realize profits.

Prompt: "Act as a business validation strategist who helps entrepreneurs move from idea to viable opportunity. My business idea is [DESCRIBE YOUR IDEA IN DETAIL]. Evaluate it across five dimensions: market demand (is there a hungry audience?), target audience clarity (who specifically would buy this?), competitive landscape (who else does this and what's my edge?), monetization potential (how and when does this make money?), and execution feasibility (what does it take to launch an MVP?). For each dimension, rate the idea's strength (strong/moderate/weak) and provide specific recommendations to strengthen weak areas. Be honest—if the idea needs pivoting, say so and suggest directions."

Technique applied: *Role priming + multi-dimensional validation + honest assessment.*

Market and Customer Research

Traditional market research used to take months and required resources. Today, AI compresses it into days, hours, or even minutes, depending on how fast you want to work on it. AI can assist with customer persona creation, predicting and mapping pain points, buying behavior analysis, and objection forecasting. This reveals any hidden opportunities and potential bottlenecks, so you eventually invest in a business with a hungry market that's ready to buy.

Prompt: "Act as a customer research strategist helping a new [INDUSTRY] business understand its buyers. My business idea is [DESCRIBE YOUR BUSINESS IDEA AND OFFER]. Create three detailed customer personas, each representing a distinct buyer type. For each, include demographics, motivations (why they'd seek this solution), frustrations (what's failing them now), buying triggers (what pushes them from interest to purchase), objections (what would make them hesitate), and preferred discovery channels (how they'd find me). Base personas on realistic market behavior, not idealizations. Highlight which persona represents the highest-value early adopter I should target first."

Technique applied: *Role priming + behavioral persona design + prioritization.*

Business Model and Business Plan Development

Even if you don't have a working structure yet, AI can help you move from chaos to decision-ready. It can draft business models, revenue streams, pricing strategies, cost structures, and risk analysis.

Prompt: "Act as a startup adviser specializing in lean business planning for [INDUSTRY]. My business idea is [DESCRIBE YOUR IDEA], targeting [AUDIENCE] with [OFFER]. Help me create a lean business plan that includes: value proposition, customer segments, revenue streams (with pricing rationale), cost structure (fixed and variable), key assumptions I'm making, top three risks and how to mitigate them, and a 90-day launch road map with milestones. Keep it decision-ready and concise—this should fit on two to three pages, not fifty. Flag which assumptions I should validate first before investing significant resources."

Technique applied: *Role priming + assumption-driven planning + risk prioritization.*

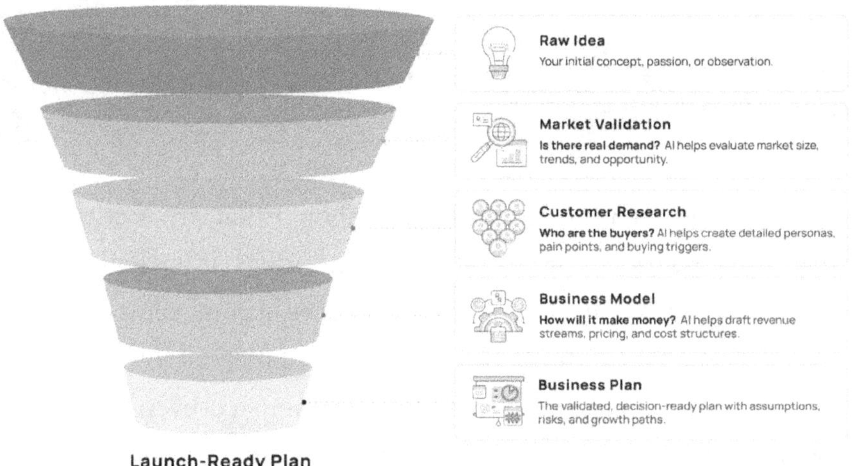

Improving Your Business

Understanding and Applying the 80/20 Rule

The Pareto principle, first identified by economist Vilfredo Pareto, states that roughly 80% of outcomes come from 20% of causes (Tardi, 2025). This pattern has since been empirically observed across business contexts in large organizations that focus on getting 80% of profits, productivity, or efficiency from 20% of customers, effort, or resources.

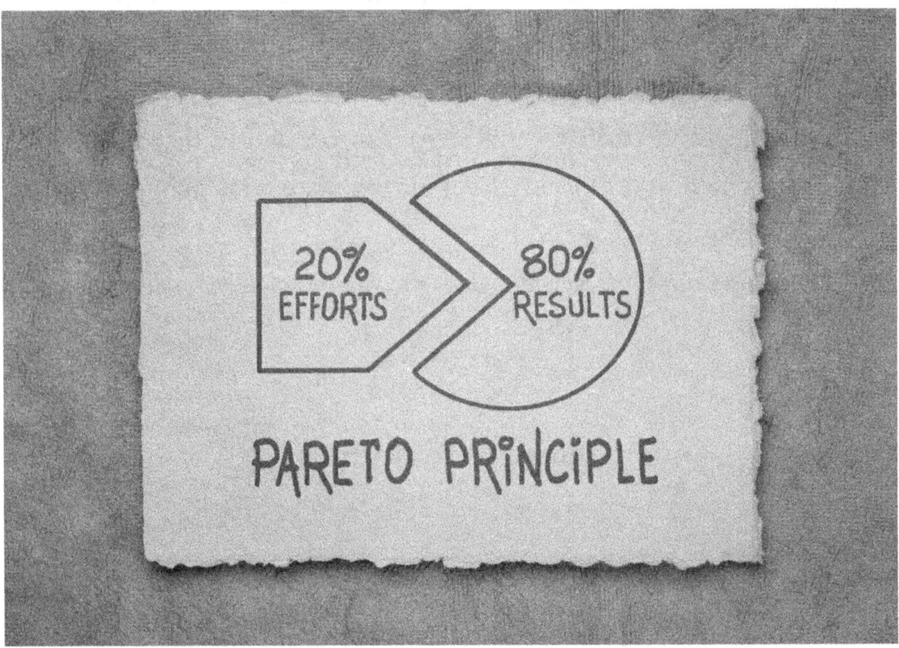

Harvard Business Review has repeatedly shown that product portfolios exhibit extreme profit concentration (Anand, 2008). McKinsey research demonstrates that complexity beyond a certain point destroys margin (Jerenz et al., 2024). The key insight is that most businesses are unintentionally optimized for activity, not impact, even though they know it should be the other way around. AI allows leaders to quantify Pareto effects instead of guessing.

AI can analyze your revenue by product, profit by client, and time spent vs. return. With effective prompting, it can help you identify low-value tasks, automate repetitive work, streamline operations, and personalize marketing at scale. The idea is to focus your energy on strategic thinking and channel your resources toward income-generating activities.

Prompt: "Act as a business efficiency consultant specializing in Pareto analysis for [INDUSTRY]. My business [BUSINESS NAME AND TYPE] generates revenue from [LIST PRODUCTS/SERVICES WITH APPROXIMATE REVENUE EACH], with a team of [NUMBER]. My most time-consuming activities are [LIST 5–10]. Apply the 80/20 rule across three dimensions: revenue by product/service, profit by client segment, and time spent vs. return. Identify the top 20% driving 80% of results and the bottom 20% consuming disproportionate resources. Recommend what to double down on, automate, delegate, or eliminate. If I've attached data [REVENUE REPORT/TIME TRACKING/CLIENT LIST], base the analysis on it. Distinguish between "low revenue now but strategic" vs. "low revenue and should go.""

***Technique applied**: Role priming + data-driven decomposition + action-oriented output.*

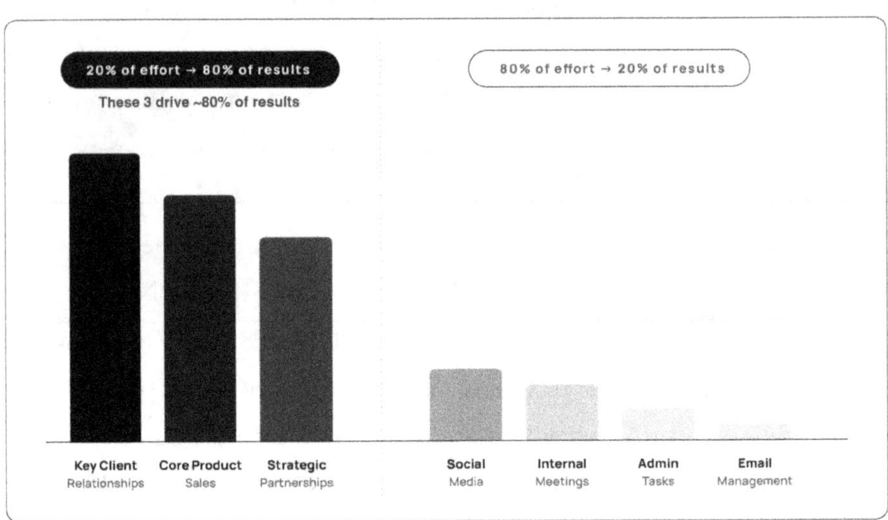

Measuring ROI and Success

Before eliminating anything you suspect to be the cause of your slowdown, you must measure reality and avoid any guesswork. AI can analyze revenue by product, service, or offer; profitability by customer segment; time spent vs. return; and acquisition cost vs. lifetime value.

A case study of one of the reputable tech companies demonstrates this: Adobe shifted from fragmented product sales to subscription-based analytics. By focusing on high-retention customers, they dramatically increased lifetime value and stabilized revenue, proving that optimization beats expansion (*Lessons From Adobe's Shift to Subscriptions*, 2025).

Prompt: "Act as a fractional CFO conducting a profitability audit for [BUSINESS TYPE]. My business [BUSINESS NAME] offers [LIST PRODUCTS/SERVICES WITH APPROXIMATE REVENUE], serving customer segments [DESCRIBE MAIN GROUPS]. If available, I've attached [REVENUE BREAKDOWN/P&L/TIME TRACKING]. Identify which products and customer segments generate the highest revenue

AND profit margin, highlight mismatches (high-revenue/low-margin items, high-effort/low-return clients), and estimate acquisition cost vs. lifetime value per segment. Recommend where to invest more, raise prices, or exit. Present as a revenue-profit matrix table and customer profitability ranking with three to five strategic recommendations. Distinguish between revenue and profit, flag confidence levels where data is incomplete."

Technique applied: *Role priming + financial decomposition + recommendation clarity.*

Eliminating Low-Profit Tasks, Products, and Clients

One of the hardest leadership disciplines is subtraction. Downsizing or eliminating some of the usual activities or products can seem as if you're failing, whereas it could be a strategic move that leads to efficiency or higher impact over time. Many studies support this: Both HBR and Bain mention that losing the bottom 10–20% of customers (and focusing on loyal, long-standing ones) often increases overall profitability (Gallo, 2014).

Understandably, this is a draining and often emotional decision to make. Since AI has no emotions (which can be both good and bad), in this case, it can help you detach emotionally and decide rationally. If you have to get rid of some employees, clients, projects, or products that would cost you money, time, or peace of mind to keep, AI can help you see this from a neutral, business-centric perspective.

Prompt: "Act as a profitability-focused business consultant for [INDUSTRY]. My business [BUSINESS NAME] currently offers [LIST PRODUCTS/SERVICES] and serves [DESCRIBE CLIENT TYPES]. I suspect that some tasks, clients, or products are draining resources without adequate return [LIST ANY SUSPECTS IF KNOWN]. Identify which items are low-profit or loss-generating and categorize each into one of four actions: eliminate entirely, restructure the delivery model, reprice to reflect true value, or transition to a lower-cost service tier. For each recommendation, explain the financial and operational impact of the change, and suggest how to communicate it to affected clients or teams without damaging relationships. Be direct—avoiding hard decisions is often more expensive than making them."

Technique applied: *Role priming + categorized action framework + communication strategy.*

Automating Repetitive Tasks

You can improve your business efficiency and operations simply by automating repetitive tasks and diverting your attention and resources to strategic or high-impact activities. AI can automate reporting, draft communications, handle routine customer queries, and streamline internal workflows.

Prompt: "Act as a business automation strategist for a [INDUSTRY] company with [TEAM SIZE] employees. My current operational tasks include [LIST KEY RECURRING TASKS], and I use [CURRENT TOOLS AND PLATFORMS]. Identify which tasks are candidates for full automation, partial automation, or delegation. For each, recommend a specific tool or workflow (e.g., Zapier, Make, AI assistants, CRM automations), estimate the time saved per week, and note the implementation difficulty (easy/medium/complex). Prioritize by highest time savings with lowest implementation effort. Present as an automation opportunity table: Task \ Current Time Spent \ Automation Type \ Recommended Tool \ Time Saved \ Difficulty."

Technique applied: *Role priming + tool-specific recommendations + effort-impact prioritization.*

An example of automation at scale is the thousands of Shopify-based businesses using AI to automate customer support, order management, and marketing workflows, freeing founders to focus on growth and partnerships instead of inbox management.

Personalizing Marketing at Scale

Accenture research shows that 91% of consumers are more likely to buy from brands that recognize and personalize experiences (*Widening Gap Between Consumer Expectations and Reality,* 2018). Customization ensures that clients feel seen, valued, and treated like they're the only customers, not part of a large group. This indicates the importance of bringing a personal touch or adding significant details unique to each customer.

While personalization can be tedious for bigger companies, AI simplifies it through segmented messaging, dynamic offers, and personalized customer journeys.

Prompt: "Act as a customer engagement strategist specializing in segmented messaging for [INDUSTRY]. My business [BUSINESS NAME AND CORE OFFER] serves three segments: [SEGMENT 1: description], [SEGMENT 2: description], [SEGMENT 3: description]. I communicate via [EMAIL/SMS/SOCIAL/IN-APP] in a [BRAND VOICE DESCRIPTION] tone, with access to [PURCHASE HISTORY/BROWSING BEHAVIOR/CRM DATA]. For each segment, create a personalized message with the behavioral trigger that activates it (e.g., post-purchase, cart abandonment, re-engagement), one personalization variable beyond the name, and a clear single CTA. Include an A/B test variation for the highest-value segment. Messages must feel personal, not template-generated."

Technique applied: *Role priming + behavioral trigger mapping + personalization depth.*

Optimizing Sales and Boosting Customer Engagement

AI can help your sales team to analyze win or loss patterns, identify high-converting messaging, and predict churn risks. With advanced analytics in sales, you can see how customers interact with your products or communication channels. AI can identify areas of engagement, confusion, hesitation, drop-off, or positive action throughout the entire sales funnel.

Prompt: "Act as a senior sales operations analyst specializing in pipeline optimization for [INDUSTRY]. My [B2B/B2C/HYBRID] business [BUSINESS NAME] sells [CORE OFFER] with an average deal size of [AMOUNT]. My pipeline stages are [LIST, e.g., Lead > Qualified > Demo > Proposal > Close] with a current conversion rate of [OVERALL OR BY STAGE, IF KNOWN]. My biggest concern is [WHERE DEALS STALL]. Identify the top three bottlenecks by stage, quantify the likely drop-off impact, diagnose root causes, and recommend specific fixes (process changes, messaging adjustments, or tools). Suggest one pipeline metric I should track weekly that I'm probably not tracking. Present as a pipeline audit table (Stage \ Conversion Rate \ Bottleneck \ Root Cause \ Fix \ Priority) with three quick wins for this week and one structural change for the next 30 days."

Technique applied: *Role priming + stage-by-stage diagnostic + action prioritization.*

Building Loyal Fans (Not Just Customers)

According to Frederick Reichheld's Net Promoter research, increasing retention by 5% can increase profits by 25–95% (Reichheld, 2001). If you can manage to keep your existing customers satisfied and feeling valued, you can even make more money than would be possible by acquiring new ones. Never underestimate the power of happy customers, because they're often your raving fans and free marketers who can refer others to your business. AI can help identify emotional loyalty drivers, repeat purchase triggers, and advocacy opportunities.

Prompt: "Act as a customer retention strategist specializing in loyalty-driven growth for [INDUSTRY]. My [B2B/B2C] business [BUSINESS NAME AND CORE OFFER] has a retention rate of [% OR "UNKNOWN"] and a repeat purchase rate of [% OR "UNKNOWN"]. What my best customers have in common is [DESCRIBE IF KNOWN], and I have access to [PURCHASE HISTORY/NPS SCORES/REVIEWS/SUPPORT TICKETS]. Identify the top five drivers of repeat purchases and emotional loyalty, explaining the psychological mechanism behind each (habit formation, identity alignment, switching cost, etc.). Suggest three retention strategies implementable within 30 days and design a simple advocacy program that turns fans into referrers. Focus on emotional loyalty (they choose you), not transactional loyalty (they're locked in). Strategies must be practical for a [BUSINESS SIZE] business."

Technique applied: *Role priming + psychological grounding + size-appropriate constraints.*

Enhancing Branding and Market Positioning

Brand Identity and Brand Statement

A strong brand identity answers one question clearly: "Why should I choose you over alternatives?" Customers want a brand that aligns with their values and cares for the things they care about. AI can help you to articulate your brand's purpose, promise, and differentiation logic. It can identify unique gaps to capitalize on to rise above competition or even help you frame your message in a way that resonates with your customers.

Prompt: "Act as a brand strategist specializing in competitive differentiation for [INDUSTRY]. My business [BUSINESS NAME AND WHAT YOU DO] serves [PRIMARY CUSTOMER SEGMENT], competing against [TOP 3 COMPETITORS]. Customers currently say [REVIEWS, FEEDBACK, OR PERCEPTION], and I want to be known for [YOUR ASPIRATION]. Define a brand identity framework covering purpose, promise, and personality. Craft a brand statement (one to two sentences) and test it against my competitors—does it differentiate? Suggest three ways to embed this identity into customer touchpoints. The statement must pass the "could a competitor say this?" test. Avoid abstract words like "innovative," "passionate," or "dedicated." Ground the identity in customer value, not self-praise."

Technique applied: *Role priming + competitive differentiation test + anti-generic constraints.*

Brand Personality Traits, Messaging, and Story

A brand with consistent personality traits can enjoy higher trust and recall. You want to ensure that customers see your brand personality through its messaging and interactions. This is why you might see behemoth companies now having social media accounts and interacting with users online to demonstrate their understanding and awareness of what happens in the world. AI can translate abstract values into language, maintain tone consistency, and align messaging across platforms.

Brand SWOT Analysis

Since AI excels at structured frameworks, it can analyze your brand's strengths, weaknesses, opportunities, and threats and help you reframe your positioning as required.

Prompt: "Act as a brand strategy consultant conducting a SWOT analysis for [BUSINESS NAME] in [INDUSTRY]. My business [WHAT YOU DO AND WHO YOU SERVE] is positioned as a [CHALLENGER/ESTABLISHED/NICHE LEADER/NEW ENTRANT]. My perceived strengths are [LIST 2–3], known vulnerabilities are [LIST 1–2], and

I'm observing these market shifts: [LIST 1–2]. Conduct a full SWOT with three to five items per quadrant, then cross-reference to extract two offensive strategies (strengths × opportunities) and two defensive strategies (weaknesses × threats). Recommend the single highest-impact strategic move. Be specific to my business, challenge whether my stated strengths are real differentiators, and flag blind spots. Defensive strategies must include a specific action with a timeline and not just awareness or monitoring. Present as a SWOT grid and strategy extraction table."

Technique applied: *Role priming + structured framework + strategic cross-referencing.*

Positioning Strategy and Value Proposition

A competitive advantage often comes from being different, not necessarily from being better at everything. You want to ensure that your brand aligns and that customers see your value portrayed effectively. AI helps you to clarify value propositions, avoid generic positioning, and anchor pricing to value.

Prompt: "Act as a value proposition specialist for [INDUSTRY] businesses. My current value proposition is [PASTE YOUR VERSION], targeting [PRIMARY AUDIENCE AND THEIR #1 PRIORITY]. The core outcome I deliver is [MAIN RESULT], and my top competitor's proposition is [PASTE OR DESCRIBE]. Evaluate mine on clarity, specificity, and differentiation (score each 1–10 with explanation). Score honestly, where at least one variation should score below 5 on at least one criterion to ensure your scoring actually discriminates between options. Rewrite in three variations: outcome-focused, pain-focused, and aspiration-focused, each in two sentences maximum. Recommend which to lead with and where to use each (homepage, pitch, elevator conversation). The final version must not be interchangeable with any competitor's messaging."

Technique applied: *Role priming + evaluative scoring + multi-angle rewriting.*

Building a Competitive Edge

Competitor Deep Dive and Strategic Gaps

Successful businesses are aware of their competitors and use that knowledge to their advantage. AI can be helpful when you need to perform a competitor deep dive and strategic gap analysis. It can analyze competitor offerings, pricing structures, messaging patterns, and customer reviews. One of the successful businesses that took advantage of strategic gaps is Netflix. It used data-driven analysis to identify content gaps competitors ignored, leading to original content strategies that redefined the industry.

Prompt: "Act as a competitive intelligence analyst specializing in [INDUSTRY]. My business is [BUSINESS NAME, OFFER, AND POSITIONING]. My top competitors are [COMPETITOR 1, 2, 3—include URLs or key details], and my perceived advantage is [WHAT I DO BETTER]. Analyze each competitor across positioning, pricing, messaging, customer experience, and product gaps. Identify three strategic gaps (unserved needs, overlooked segments, messaging blind spots) and assess each by opportunity size, difficulty to capture, and what it would take. Recommend two moves I should make within 90 days. Base analysis on publicly observable signals, distinguish real gaps from gaps that exist for a reason, and present as a competitor table with an opportunity ranking."

Technique applied: *Role priming + multi-dimensional competitor analysis + action-oriented output.*

Extracting Competitor Strategies

AI can help reverse-engineer winning business models, go-to-market approaches, funnel structures, and value ladders. While most businesses protect their trade secrets, they often leave their success trail through announcements, acquisitions, ads, and customer reviews. Therefore, if there's any company whose success you want to emulate, you can feed it into an AI model and prompt it to map out how it derives its success. AI can scrape publicly available information regarding that company, analyze it, and even predict undisclosed strategies the company might be using.

Scaling Your Business

Proper business scaling is not just about doing more but about channeling your efforts, doing less of the wrong things, and buying back your time without compromising the quality of your product or service. AI supports decision rules, priority frameworks, profit-focused analysis, and energy-aware leadership.

Mindset Shift

A mindset shift in the AI era can differentiate you from the competition through working smarter, not harder. Since productivity doesn't necessarily scale linearly with hours worked, strategic focus can outperform effort. You being here, reading this book right now or binging on AI techniques and the latest tools, while others are still skeptical of integrating AI into their organizations, is proof that you have a flexible, growth mindset. If you can shift your mindset to learn effective prompting techniques, imagine how far you can scale your business!

Focus on Growth Beyond Revenue Increase

It's important to note that fixating your team on revenue growth without considering margin and systems might lead to burnout. There are other ways in which your organization can experience scalable growth. AI can help you to track profitable growth, spot fragile expansion, and build resilience. It can also help you to identify scaling opportunities you might have been missing.

Prompt: "Act as a business growth strategist for a [STARTUP/GROWTH/MATURE] company in [INDUSTRY] with [AMOUNT] annual revenue and a team of [NUMBER]. My biggest operational challenge is [DESCRIBE] and I currently focus on [REVENUE/CUSTOMER COUNT/OTHER] as my primary metric. Identify five non-revenue growth measures I should track: operational efficiency, customer health metrics, team capacity, brand equity indicators, and strategic positioning. For each, specify the exact metric to track, a benchmark to aim for in [INDUSTRY], and one action I can take this quarter. Prioritize measures that compound over time, avoid vanity metrics, and present as a growth dashboard framework."

Technique applied: *Role priming + multi-dimensional growth analysis + actionable benchmarking.*

Identifying Low-Value and Energy-Draining Tasks

Sometimes, business growth can happen when you ditch the low-value, resource-consuming activities and rechannel your efforts strategically.

Prompt: "Act as a business operations auditor specializing in time-value optimization. My role is [TITLE AND CORE RESPONSIBILITIES], working approximately [HOURS] hours weekly. Tasks I suspect are low-value include [LIST 3–5], and I use [MAIN TOOLS AND PLATFORMS]. Categorize my tasks into four quadrants: High Value + Energizing, High Value + Draining, Low Value + Energizing, Low Value

+ Draining. For each low-value task, recommend whether to automate (with specific tool suggestions), delegate (with role suggestions), simplify, or eliminate. Estimate realistic hours recovered per week from each change. Present as a task audit matrix and action table (Task \ Time Spent \ Recommendation \ Tool/Process \ Hours Recovered)."

Technique applied: *Role priming + quadrant analysis + tool-specific recommendations.*

This kind of prompt often works best with attached files or linked knowledge base material for AI to assess. AI can quickly spot tasks that can be automated, delegated, or replaced and suggest a different resource allocation for high efficiency.

Prioritizing Profitable Activities and Clients

Similarly, AI can help shift your focus and resources toward income-generating activities and prioritize profitable clients.

Prompt: "Act as a profitability strategist for a [BUSINESS TYPE] with [TEAM SIZE] employees. My products/services are [LIST WITH REVENUE AND ESTIMATED MARGIN], serving client segments [DESCRIBE TOP 3–4 TYPES] with a revenue split of approximately [% BY PRODUCT OR CLIENT]. My biggest scalability bottleneck is [WHAT LIMITS GROWTH]. Rank products by revenue, margin, and scalability; rank clients by lifetime value, cost to serve, retention, and referral likelihood. Identify the "golden intersection": product-client combinations with the highest profitability AND scalability and recommend what to invest in, maintain, or phase out. Separate "profitable now" from "scalable later" and be direct about what to deprioritize."

Technique applied: *Role priming + dual-axis ranking + strategic focus constraints.*

Establishing Decision Rules

Most high-performing organizations rely more on rules than on constant decisions. This is why they often operate with structured and solid methodologies. AI brings clarity and formalizes go or no-go criteria, investment thresholds, and client acceptance rules.

Prompt: "Act as a strategic operations adviser who builds decision frameworks for growing businesses. My business is at the [STARTUP/GROWTH/MATURE] stage with [REVENUE] and a team of [NUMBER] at [UTILIZATION LEVEL]. My biggest decision challenge is [TAKING ON TOO MANY CLIENTS/SAYING YES TO WRONG PROJECTS/UNCLEAR EXPANSION CRITERIA], and a past mistake was [DESCRIBE AND WHY]. Create go/no-go decision frameworks for three categories: new client acceptance, project evaluation, and expansion opportunities. For each, provide three to five measurable criteria, a scoring mechanism, a "red flag" list for automatic rejection, and one example of how it would have changed a past decision. Keep rules simple enough for any team member to apply consistently, and present as ready-to-use checklists."

Technique applied: *Role priming + framework design + scenario validation.*

Key Takeaways

- AI can serve as a career architect by helping you clarify goals, evaluate skills against market demands, create personalized learning paths, build a personal brand, and prepare powerful resumes and interview strategies.
- Starting a new business is accelerated with AI support for validating ideas, conducting market and customer research, and developing comprehensive business models and business plans.

- The 80/20 rule (Pareto Principle) applied with AI analysis helps businesses identify the 20% of activities, products, and clients that drive 80% of results, enabling focused resource allocation and elimination of low-value tasks.
- Branding, market positioning, and competitive analysis are strengthened through AI-assisted brand identity development, SWOT analysis, value proposition refinement, and competitor strategy extraction.
- Scaling a business requires a mindset shift supported by AI, from identifying low-value tasks to automate or delegate, to establishing decision rules and prioritizing high-impact growth activities beyond simple revenue increase.

CHAPTER

PROMPT LIBRARY

While this book contains specific sections that help you comprehend the prompting techniques fully, this chapter is full of tested and best-performing prompts. It's a ready-to-execute, production-grade prompt library designed for SMBs, industry leaders, and professionals across major industries. Each prompt uses one or more of the advanced prompt engineering techniques discussed in earlier chapters. As a prompting hero, you can now leverage role priming, context anchoring, constraints, step-by-step reasoning, audience targeting, output formatting, and performance optimization with the aid of AI. Observe the library follows a specific structure that repeats in every prompt on purpose (adding role, context, task, and constraints). This provides an AI model with sufficient details on which to base its output. Most LLMs can capture your intent from this prompt structure, even if you don't use full sentences. Try this basic structure first, and once you understand it, and the outputs you get, you can start tweaking them based on your goals, using all the methods you've learned in the previous chapters. Think of those as starting points, not a final, rigid set.

To effectively use this library, copy a prompt from the role and add constraints or customize the bracketed fields [] as needed. You can run the edited prompt as is in your AI tool of choice, such as ChatGPT, Claude, or Perplexity. Don't forget to apply deep research (or thinking mode) whenever you need more insightful outputs or when fast mode doesn't suffice.

ANATOMY OF A STRUCTURED PROMPT

Role

What it does: Tells the AI who to be. Defines the expertise, perspective, and authority level.

You're a senior brand strategist with 15+ years of experience helping [BUSINESS] dominate competitive markets.

Business Context

What it does: Gives the AI the background it needs. Industry, audience, offer, positioning, competitors.

Industry, Target Audience, Core Offer, Price Positioning, Key Competitors

Task

What it does: Tells the AI exactly what to produce. Specific, numbered deliverables.

1) Define brand positioning statement.
2) Identify unique value proposition.
3) Create brand voice guide.
4) Generate three messaging pillars with proof points.

Constraints

What it does: Sets boundaries on what to avoid and how to format the output.

Avoid generic clichés. Focus on clarity and customer relevance. Output in clean, scannable sections.

Marketing and Branding Prompts

Brand Positioning Messaging Prompt

Role: You're a senior brand strategist with 15+ years of experience helping [BUSINESS] dominate competitive markets in [GOAL].

Business context:

- Industry [INDUSTRY]
- Target audience [IDEAL CUSTOMER]
- Core offer [PRODUCT/SERVICE]
- Price positioning [BUDGET/MID/PREMIUM]
- Key competitors [COMPETITORS]

Task:

1. Define a clear brand positioning statement.
2. Identify a unique value proposition that differentiates this business.

3. Create a brand voice guide (tone, personality, words to use, and words to avoid).
4. Generate three messaging pillars with supporting proof points.

Constraints:

- Avoid generic marketing clichés [WHAT TO AVOID].
- Focus on clarity and customer relevance.
- Output in clean, scannable sections.

Technique: *Role priming + constraint layering*

A quality response might include: a clear positioning statement with competitive differentiation, a structured brand voice guide with specific word lists, and three messaging pillars grounded in customer pain points.

High-Converting Marketing Campaign Prompt

Role: Act as a performance marketing director specializing in [BUSINESS] growth campaigns.

Context: Campaign details:

- Goal [LEADS/SALES/AWARENESS]
- Channel [EMAIL/SOCIAL/ADS/CONTENT]
- Audience awareness level [COLD/WARM/HOT]
- Budget range [LOW/MEDIUM/HIGH]

Task:

- Campaign concept and hook
- Core message framework
- CTA strategy
- Three headline options

- Three body copy variations optimized for conversion
- Explain why each element works psychologically.

Technique: *Role priming + structured output*

A quality response might include: a campaign concept with a psychological hook, message framework mapped to awareness level, and copy variations with explained persuasion mechanics.

Product Launch Go-to-Market Prompt

Role: Act as a senior go-to-market strategist with experience launching products in [INDUSTRY].

Context:

- Product [PRODUCT NAME AND DESCRIPTION]
- Target market [ICP/AUDIENCE]
- Launch timeline [WEEKS/MONTHS]
- Budget [RANGE]
- Competitive landscape [KEY COMPETITORS]

Task:

- Define launch phases (pre-launch, launch, post-launch) with specific activities per phase
- Identify the primary and secondary channels with budget allocation rationale
- Create a messaging matrix: core message, proof points, and objection responses per audience segment

Constraints:

- Tie every activity to a measurable KPI
- Include a contingency plan for the top two launch risks

- Present as a timeline-based action plan with owner placeholders

Technique: *Role priming + phased planning + contingency design.*

A quality response might include: a three-phase launch plan with specific activities and KPIs, channel strategy with budget rationale, and a messaging matrix segmented by audience.

Sales and Lead Generation

Sales Script and Objection Handling Prompt

Role: You're a top-performing B2B sales consultant.

Sales context:

- Product/service [OFFER]
- Sales model [CALL/EMAIL/DM/IN-PERSON]
- Average deal size [AMOUNT]
- Common objections [LIST]

Task:

- A full sales script from opening to close
- Tailored responses to each objection
- Soft-close and hard-close options

Constraints - Style rules:

- Conversational, confident, non-pushy
- Emphasize value over price

Technique: *Role priming + scenario-based generation.*

A quality response might include: a conversational script with natural transitions from opening to close, tailored objection responses that reframe value, and distinct soft-close vs. hard-close language.

Lead Magnet Creation Prompt

Role: Act as a demand-generation strategist for SMBs [BUSINESS].

Context:

- Target market [NICHE]
- Main pain point [PAIN POINT/PROBLEM]
- Desired outcome [RESULT]

Task:

- Five lead magnet ideas
- Recommended format for each (PDF, checklist, quiz, email course) [SELECT]
- Funnel placement strategy
- Follow-up nurture sequence outline (five steps)

Technique: *Role priming + multi-output generation.*

A quality response might include: five distinct lead magnet concepts matched to the pain point, format recommendations with rationale, and a nurture sequence with clear progression logic.

Operations and Process Optimization

SOP Creation Prompt

Role: You're an operations manager hired to document and optimize business processes.

Context:

- Process to document [PROCESS NAME]
- Business size [TEAM SIZE]
- Tools used [TOOLS]

Task: Deliver an SOP including:

- Purpose and success criteria
- Step-by-step workflow
- Roles and responsibilities
- Common errors and prevention tips
- KPIs to track
- Format for easy handover to new employees.

Technique: *Role priming + structured decomposition.*

A quality response might include: a clear purpose statement, numbered step-by-step workflows with decision points, role assignments, and measurable KPIs for each process stage.

Automation Opportunities Prompt

Role: Act as a meticulous business automation consultant.

Context:

- Industry [INDUSTRY]
- Repetitive tasks [TASK LIST]
- Current tools [TOOLS]

Task:

- Automation opportunities
- Suggested tools or workflows
- Estimated time saved per week
- Risks and implementation notes

Technique: *Role priming + analytical decomposition.*

A quality response might include: prioritized automation candidates ranked by time savings, specific tool recommendations with integration notes, and realistic implementation risk assessments.

Finance and Strategy

Pricing Strategy Prompt

Role: You're a pricing strategist specializing in [NICHE] profitability.

Context:

- Product/service [OFFER]
- Cost structure [FIXED AND VARIABLE COSTS]
- Market type [COMMODITY/DIFFERENTIATED]
- Customer sensitivity to price [LOW/MEDIUM/HIGH]

Task:

- Three pricing models
- Pros and cons of each
- Psychological pricing recommendations
- Upsell and cross-sell opportunities

Technique: *Role priming + constraint layering.*

A quality response might include: distinct pricing tiers with pros and cons for each, psychological anchoring rationale, and upsell pathways tied to customer segments.

Financial Forecasting Prompt

Role: Act as a fractional CFO for a growing [BUSINESS].

Business data:

- Current monthly revenue [AMOUNT]
- Growth goal [TARGET]
- Time horizon [MONTHS]
- Key expenses [LIST]

Task:

- Revenue forecast scenarios (conservative, realistic, aggressive)
- Cash flow risks
- Strategic recommendations

Constraints:

- Format rules (include graphs or tables) [FORMAT]
- Avoid [SPECIFY]

Technique: *Role priming + scenario analysis.*

A quality response might include: three clearly differentiated forecast scenarios with underlying assumptions, cash flow risk factors with probability indicators, and strategic recommendations tied to each scenario.

Data Analysis and Insight Extraction Prompt

Role: Act as a senior data analyst and business intelligence strategist.

Context:

- Data description [DESCRIBE DATASET OR PASTE SUMMARY STATISTICS]
- Business question [WHAT YOU NEED TO ANSWER]

- Available tools [EXCEL/SQL/PYTHON/BI TOOL]

Task:

- Recommend the analysis approach and key metrics to examine
- Identify potential patterns, anomalies, or segments worth investigating
- Translate findings into three to five actionable business recommendations
- Constraints:
- Distinguish between correlation and causation explicitly
- Flag data quality concerns or limitations that affect confidence
- Present insights in plain business language with a technical appendix for methodology

Technique: *Role priming + analytical decomposition + epistemic humility constraints.*

A quality response might include: a clear analysis methodology, pattern identification with confidence qualifiers, and business recommendations separated from technical methodology.

Customer Experience and Retention

Customer Journey Mapping

Role: You're a first-class customer experience (CX) strategist.

Context:

- Business type [B2B/B2C]
- Main acquisition channel [CHANNEL]
- Retention challenges [ISSUES]

Task:

- Full customer journey
- Emotional states at each stage
- Friction points
- Improvement opportunities

Constraints:

- Present as a stage-by-stage table

Technique: *Role priming + stage-based decomposition.*

A quality response might include: a stage-by-stage journey from awareness to advocacy, emotional states mapped per stage, and specific friction points with actionable improvements.

Feedback and Review Strategy

Role: Act as a reputation management expert.

Inputs:

- Platform [GOOGLE/TRUSTPILOT/SOCIAL]
- Industry norms [EXPECTATIONS]

Task:

- Ethical review request scripts
- Timing strategy
- Response templates for positive and negative reviews

Constraints:

- Friendly, professional tone

Technique: *Role priming + template generation.*

A quality response might include: tactful review request scripts with optimal timing windows, response templates that address negative feedback constructively, and platform-specific best practices.

HR, Leadership, and Culture

Hiring and Interview Framework

Role: You're an HR leader helping [COMPANY] hire its next team member.

Context: Role details:

- Position [JOB TITLE]
- Required skills [SKILLS]
- Culture values [VALUES]

Task:

- Job description
- Interview questions (skills + culture)
- Scorecard for evaluation
- Red flags to watch for

Technique: *Role priming + structured evaluation design.*

A quality response might include: a job description aligned to culture values, behavioral and technical interview questions with scoring rubrics, and red flag indicators tied to role requirements.

Performance Management Prompt

Role: Act as a high-grade leadership coach for [COMPANY/ DEPARTMENT].

Context:

- Team size [NUMBER]
- Performance issue [ISSUE]

Task:

- Diagnosis of root causes
- Performance improvement plan
- Communication framework
- Motivation strategies

Constraints:

- Structure as numbered action plan

Technique: *Role priming + diagnostic framework.*

A quality response might include: root cause analysis of the performance issue, a phased improvement plan with milestones, and communication scripts for difficult conversations.

Strategy and Growth

Business Growth Road Map Prompt

Role: You're a strategic growth adviser.

Context: Business snapshot:

- Current stage [START-UP/GROWTH/MATURE]
- Revenue [AMOUNT]

- Core constraint [LIMITATION]

Task:

- 12-month growth road map
- Priority initiatives
- Key metrics per quarter
- Risk mitigation plan

Technique: *Role priming + temporal planning.*

A quality response might include: quarterly milestones with specific KPIs, prioritized initiatives ranked by impact and feasibility, and risk mitigation strategies tied to the core constraint.

Competitive Analysis Prompt

Role: Act as a competitive intelligence analyst.

Inputs:

- Market [MARKET]
- Top competitors [LIST/URLs]
- Industry [INDUSTRY]
- Your business position [YOUR POSITION/STRENGTHS]

Task:

- Strengths and weaknesses
- Positioning gaps
- Opportunities for differentiation
- Strategic recommendations

Constraints:

- Present as a comparison table with one row per competitor

Technique: *Role priming + comparative analysis.*

A quality response might include: a structured competitor comparison across key dimensions, positioning gaps with exploitable opportunities, and differentiation strategies grounded in market data.

Negotiation Preparation Prompt

Role: Act as a senior negotiation strategist with expertise in high-stakes business deals.

Context:

- Negotiation type [CONTRACT/PARTNERSHIP/SALARY/VENDOR/M&A]
- Your position [DESCRIBE YOUR SIDE]
- Counterparty [DESCRIBE THEIR POSITION AND KNOWN PRIORITIES]
- Your ideal outcome [BEST CASE]
- Your walk-away point [MINIMUM ACCEPTABLE]

Task:

- Map both parties' interests, priorities, and likely pressure points
- Develop three negotiation scenarios (aggressive, balanced, concession-heavy) with scripted talking points for each
- Identify two to three leverage points and two to three concessions you can offer that cost you little but hold high perceived value

Constraints:

- Be strategically honest — avoid manipulative tactics
- Ground recommendations in negotiation frameworks (BATNA, ZOPA, anchoring)
- Present as a preparation brief with a quick-reference cheat sheet

Technique: *Role priming + scenario modeling + framework application.*

A quality response might include: a dual-perspective interest map, three scripted negotiation scenarios, and a quick-reference cheat sheet with leverage points and strategic concessions.

Writing, Editing, and Formatting

Content Writing Prompts

Executive Draft Report

Role: You're a leading professional business writer specializing in [NICHE] (e.g., B2B, real estate, personal finance, etc.).

Task: Produce a structured draft report on [TOPIC]. Include:

- Executive summary (three paragraphs)
- Key findings
- Strategic recommendations
- Risks and mitigation

Constraints:

- Use a formal business tone [HBR/MCKINSEY]
- Include verifiable citations in [APA/MLA/CHICAGO/STYLE]
- Avoid unfounded claims

Technique: *Role priming + structured output with citation constraints.*

A quality response might include: a concise executive summary, evidence-backed findings with proper citations, and actionable recommendations with risk assessments.

Copywriting

Role: Act as a matchless email copywriter with industry flair.

Task: Write five personalized outreach email templates for [INDUSTRY SEGMENT]. Each should include:

- Unique opening based on company context (e.g., hiring growth, recent funding, product update)
- Specific value proposition (retention, efficiency, compliance)
- Concise, low-friction CTA

Example:

Email [RECIPIENT ADDRESS]

Subject [SUBJECT]

Hi [CLIENT'S FIRST NAME],

I noticed [COMPANY NAME] has been scaling rapidly, especially with [SPECIFIC SIGNAL/EXPANSION/FUNDING].

Teams at this stage often struggle with [CORE PAIN POINT], which quietly slows momentum just when speed matters most.

I help [INDUSTRY SEGMENT] teams use [YOUR SOLUTION] to [SPECIFIC OUTCOME/MEASURABLE RESULT] without adding complexity.

Open to a 15-minute conversation to see if this is relevant for [COMPANY NAME] right now?

Best regards,

Jane Smith [YOUR NAME]

Technique: *Role priming + example-driven generation.*

A quality response might include: five distinct email templates with personalized openings, value propositions tailored to different signals, and low-friction CTAs that feel conversational.

Proofreading and Editing Prompts

Role: You're a meticulous editor with 20 years of proofreading and editing experience.

Context: [INSERT DOCUMENT/TEXT]

Task: Review this document for formatting consistency:

- Heading levels (H1, H2, H3)
- Bulleted lists
- Citation style (APA/MLA/Chicago)
- Return a version ready for publishing.

Technique: *Role priming + checklist-based review.*

A quality response might include: *systematic formatting corrections organized by category, consistent heading hierarchy, and a publication-ready clean version.*

Social Media Prompts

Brand Visual Concept Generator

Role: Act as a senior brand strategist and visual director with experience in commercial design and brand systems.

Context:

- Industry [INDUSTRY]
- Brand personality (e.g., bold, calm, premium) [BRAND TONE]
- Target audience [AUDIENCE]
- Primary use case (web, pitch deck, ads) [USE CASE]
- Color/style preferences [PREFERENCE]

Task: Generate a brand-aligned image concept that visually represents:

- The brand's core value proposition
- Target audience appeal
- Emotional tone and market positioning
- The image should be suitable for use in marketing, presentations, or digital platforms.

Constraints:

- Avoid abstract or surreal imagery unless explicitly requested
- Maintain commercial, professional aesthetics
- Ensure visual clarity at multiple sizes
- Align with brand tone and industry norms

Technique: *Role priming + multi-dimensional constraint layering.*

A quality response might include: a detailed visual concept brief with color palette rationale, audience-aligned imagery choices, and scalability considerations across media formats.

Brand Story Video Generator

Role: Act as a brand storytelling director for commercial video.

Context:

- Brand mission [MISSION]
- Target audience [AUDIENCE]
- Video length [LENGTH]
- Platform [LINKEDIN/LANDING PAGE/PITCH]

Task: Create a video concept that tells a clear brand story, including:

- Opening hook

- Core message
- Visual progression
- Emotional payoff

Constraints:

- Business-appropriate pacing
- Clear narrative arc
- No unnecessary cinematic effects
- Optimized for attention in the first 5 seconds

Technique: *Role priming + narrative structure.*

A quality response might include: a scene-by-scene video outline with timing cues, a clear narrative arc from hook to emotional payoff, and platform-specific format recommendations.

Static Image to Brand Motion Video (Content Repurposing)

Role: Act as a motion design lead for business content.

Context:

- Source image description [PASTE IMAGE OR DESCRIPTION]
- Motion style [SUBTLE/MODERN/CALM]
- Video length [SIZE]
- Platform [PLATFORM]

Task: Animate the image into a subtle, professional motion video that enhances engagement while preserving brand integrity.

Constraints:

- Smooth, restrained motion

- No distracting transitions
- Preserve original image composition
- Suitable for corporate platforms

Technique: *Role priming + content repurposing framework.*

A quality response might include: specific motion design directions for each image element, timing and transition notes, and platform-optimized export recommendations.

Career Planning

Role: Act as a senior career strategist and executive coach with deep experience in leadership development and future-of-work trends.

Context:

- Current role [JOB TITLE]
- Industry [INDUSTRY]
- Core interests [INTERESTS]
- Income goals (three to five years) [INCOME TARGET]
- Lifestyle preferences [REMOTE/FLEXIBLE/EXECUTIVE/ENTREPRENEURIAL]

Task: Help me clarify my ideal career direction over the next three to five years. Provide:

- Two to three viable career trajectories
- Trade-offs for each path
- A recommended primary direction with rationale

Constraints:

- Avoid generic advice

- Anchor recommendations in realistic market dynamics
- Balance ambition with sustainability
- Consider AI's impact on leadership roles.
- Account for current experience level and industry stage
- Present as side-by-side path comparison

Technique: *Role priming + scenario comparison.*

A quality response might include: two to three career trajectories with realistic trade-offs, market-informed salary and growth projections, and a recommended path with clear rationale.

Resume Reframing Prompt

Role: Act as a senior executive resume strategist.

Context: [INSERT FILE]

Task: Rewrite my resume to highlight:

- Leadership influence [SKILL]
- Strategic outcomes
- AI-driven or data-informed impact instead of task execution.

Constraints:

- Use outcome-driven bullet points
- Quantify impact where possible
- Align with senior-level expectations
- Format as ready-to-use resume bullet points

Technique: *Role priming + outcome-driven rewriting.*

A quality response might include: rewritten bullet points emphasizing strategic impact over tasks, quantified achievements, and language aligned to senior-level role expectations.

Interview Simulator

Role: Act as a senior executive interviewer and leadership assessor.

Context: I want to prepare for high-stakes interviews for senior or leadership roles [ROLE] in [INDUSTRY].

Task:

- Ask me challenging executive-level interview questions
- Evaluate my responses
- Provide direct feedback on clarity, leadership presence, and strategic thinking

Constraints:

- Ask follow-up questions
- Be constructively critical
- Assess decision-making depth and AI awareness

Technique: *Role priming + interactive simulation.*

A quality response might include: executive-level behavioral and strategic questions, real-time evaluation of response quality, and specific coaching on leadership presence and strategic articulation.

Real Estate

Buyer and Seller Lead Conversion Prompt

Role: You're a top-performing real estate growth strategist with deep knowledge of local property markets.

Context:

- Market location [CITY/AREA]

- Target client [BUYERS / SELLERS/INVESTORS]
- Property range [PRICE RANGE]
- Primary channel [SOCIAL/LISTINGS/REFERRALS]

Task:

- Craft a lead-nurture message sequence (five steps)
- Address emotional drivers (fear, urgency, trust)
- Include trust signals (local expertise, proof, credibility)

Output requirements:

- Message goal per step
- Suggested CTA
- Objection handled in each step.

Technique: *Role priming + sequential engagement design.*

A quality response might include: *a five-step message sequence with escalating commitment, emotional driver mapping per stage, and objection-handling embedded naturally in each message.*

Ecommerce

Product Page Conversion Optimization Prompt

Role: You're a senior ecommerce CRO specialist.

Context:

- Product [PRODUCT NAME]
- Target buyer persona [PERSONA]
- Price point [PRICE]
- Current conversion challenge [ISSUE]

Task:

- Optimized product page structure
- Benefit-driven headline and subheadline
- Five persuasive bullet points
- Risk-reversal strategy (guarantees, social proof)

Optimization lens:

- Customer psychology
- Objection minimization
- Mobile-first clarity

Technique: *Role priming + conversion psychology framework.*

A quality response might include: a restructured product page layout with persuasion hierarchy, benefit-driven copy replacing feature lists, and risk-reversal elements positioned at decision points.

Coaching and Consulting

Authority-Building Content Engine Prompt

Role: Act as a personal brand and thought leadership strategist for high-ticket coaches.

Context:

- Niche [COACHING NICHE]
- Core transformation [RESULT]
- Platform [LINKEDIN/INSTAGRAM/YOUTUBE]

Task:

- Ten content pillar topics

- Three authority post formats per pillar
- CTA strategy that leads to discovery calls

Style constraints:

- Confident but not hype-driven
- Insight-rich, experience-backed

Technique: *Role priming + content system design.*

A quality response might include: ten content pillars mapped to authority themes, three post formats per pillar with structural templates, and a CTA strategy that nurtures toward discovery calls.

Healthcare

Patient Trust and Acquisition Prompt

Role: You're a healthcare marketing strategist specializing in ethical patient acquisition.

Inputs:

- Practice type [DENTAL/MEDICAL/WELLNESS]
- Core services [SERVICES]
- Patient concerns [FEARS/OBJECTIONS]

Task:

- Patient journey map from awareness to booking
- Trust-building messaging at each stage
- Compliance-safe marketing recommendations

Constraints:

- Clear, compassionate language

- Avoid medical claims or exaggeration.

Technique: *Role priming + ethical constraint layering.*

A quality response might include: a patient journey from awareness to booking with trust signals at each stage, compliance-safe messaging recommendations, and compassionate language frameworks.

SaaS (B2B or B2C Software Products)

Product-Led Growth Strategy Prompt

Role: You're a SaaS growth adviser experienced in scaling subscription-based products.

Context:

- Product category [SOFTWARE TYPE]
- ICP
- Pricing model [FREEMIUM/TRIAL/PAID]
- Churn challenge [ISSUE]

Task:

- Activation strategy for new users
- In-app engagement triggers
- Upgrade nudges tied to value moments
- Retention improvement ideas

Technique: *Role priming + lifecycle-based strategy.*

A quality response might include: activation milestones tied to value realization, in-app engagement triggers mapped to user behavior, and upgrade nudges aligned with demonstrated product value.

Role-Based, Context-Rich, and Constraint-Heavy CoT Prompt

Role: Act as a senior start-up operations and organizational strategy adviser [JOB TITLE] with expertise in [INDUSTRY/NICHE].

Context: A start-up is evaluating remote work adoption.
Task: Analyze the impact of remote work [SCENARIO] on a start-up [SUBJECT] by:

1. Identifying the key benefits and risks across productivity, team communication, company culture, employee satisfaction, operational costs, and scalability [METRICS]
2. Explaining how the risks can be mitigated [RESULTS] and how the benefits can be intentionally leveraged to support sustainable growth [GOAL]
3. Recommending practical, actionable strategies for implementing remote work policies effectively in a start-up environment.
4. Deliver the analysis in a clear, structured format suitable for founders or leadership teams making strategic decisions.

Constraints:

- Avoid surface-level or generic commentary
- Focus on start-up-specific realities (limited resources, fast growth, uncertainty)
- Emphasize trade-offs and second-order effects
- Present conclusions and recommendations clearly, without exposing internal reasoning chains
- Prioritize actionable insights over theory

Technique: *Chain-of-thought + role priming + constraint layering.*

A quality response might include: a structured analysis of remote work impacts across multiple dimensions, evidence-based risk mitigation strategies, and actionable policy recommendations for start-up contexts.

PoT Prompt

Role: Act as a senior procurement strategist and operations systems designer with expertise in [NICHE].

Context: An organization needs a repeatable and defensible process for evaluating potential new suppliers.

Task: Design a detailed, step-by-step evaluation algorithm for assessing potential suppliers based on the following core criteria:

- Cost
- Reliability
- Delivery time

For each criterion, specify:

- How to collect relevant data
- How to analyze and validate that data
- How to establish benchmarks or thresholds for acceptable performance

Then:

- Define how to weight and combine the criteria to arrive at a final decision
- Explain how to handle trade-offs between cost, reliability, and delivery speed
- Include methods for verifying supplier-provided information

- Recommend how to document, score, and compare supplier evaluations in a structured and auditable way

Constraint:

- Present the output as a clear procedural algorithm that can be implemented operationally.

Technique: *Program-of-thought + procedural decomposition.*

A quality response might include: a step-by-step evaluation algorithm with data collection methods, weighted scoring criteria with trade-off handling, and an auditable comparison framework.

Advanced Technique Prompts

Schema-First Market Entry Analysis

Role: Act as a senior market strategist and structured reasoning specialist.

Context:

- Target market [MARKET/REGION]
- Product or service [OFFER]
- Entry budget [BUDGET RANGE]
- Timeline [MONTHS]

Task:

- Define an evaluation schema before generating analysis: list the dimensions you will assess (market size, regulatory environment, competitive density, cultural fit, distribution complexity, and resource requirements)
- For each dimension, provide a rating (1–5) with supporting evidence

- Synthesize findings into a go/no-go recommendation with conditions

Constraints:

- Present the schema first, then populate it — do not skip the schema step
- Anchor ratings in verifiable market signals, not assumptions
- Include a sensitivity analysis: which two factors, if changed, would flip your recommendation?

Technique: *Schema-first prompting + structured reasoning.*

A quality response might include: an explicit evaluation framework defined before analysis begins, dimension-by-dimension ratings with cited evidence, and a recommendation with clear sensitivity triggers.

RAG / Knowledge Grounding Prompt

Role: Act as a senior research analyst specializing in evidence-based business intelligence.

Context:

- Research topic [TOPIC]
- Source documents [PASTE TEXT, URLS, OR DESCRIBE SOURCES]
- Decision to inform [BUSINESS DECISION]

Task:

- Synthesize the provided source material into a structured briefing
- For every claim or recommendation, cite the specific source it draws from

- Clearly flag where source material is insufficient and additional research is needed

Constraints:

- Do not generate claims beyond what the sources support
- Separate source-grounded findings from your own inferences, labeling each clearly
- Present as a briefing document with an executive summary, key findings, evidence gaps, and recommended next steps

Technique: *Retrieval-augmented generation (knowledge grounding) + citation constraints.*

A quality response might include: a structured briefing with every claim traced to its source, clearly labeled inferences, and an evidence gaps section that prevents overconfident conclusions.

Guarded Generation (Compliance-Safe Content)

Role: Act as a senior compliance-aware content strategist with expertise in [REGULATED INDUSTRY — e.g., finance, healthcare, legal].

Context:

- Content type [BLOG/EMAIL/AD/LANDING PAGE]
- Target audience [AUDIENCE]
- Regulatory framework [FDA/FTC/SEC/HIPAA/GDPR or DESCRIBE]
- Key message to communicate [MESSAGE]

Task:

- Draft the content while proactively avoiding language that could trigger regulatory violations

- After the draft, provide a compliance self-audit: list each sentence that carries regulatory risk and explain why it is or is not compliant

Constraints:

- Never use absolute claims (e.g., "guaranteed," "proven," "cures") unless sourced and permissible
- Include required disclaimers where applicable
- Flag any section where legal review is recommended before publication

Technique: *Guarded generation + self-audit constraint.*

A quality response might include: *compliant content with prohibited language proactively avoided, a sentence-level compliance audit, and flagged sections requiring legal review.*

Iterative Refinement / Strategy Stress-Test

Role: Act as a critical strategy adviser and red-team analyst.

Context:

- Strategy or plan to stress-test [PASTE STRATEGY OR DESCRIBE]
- Industry [INDUSTRY]
- Stakeholders affected [STAKEHOLDERS]

Task:

- Round 1: Identify the three strongest assumptions in the strategy and challenge each with a realistic counter-scenario
- Round 2: For each vulnerability found, propose a mitigation or pivot

- Round 3: Rewrite the strategy's executive summary incorporating the strongest improvements

Constraints:

- Be genuinely critical — do not default to validation
- Ground counter-scenarios in real market dynamics, not hypotheticals
- Present each round as a distinct section so the refinement progression is visible

Technique: *Iterative refinement + adversarial prompting.*

A quality response might include: three rounds of progressively sharper analysis, counter-scenarios grounded in market realities, and a rewritten executive summary that is demonstrably stronger than the original.

Context Compression Prompt

Role: Act as a senior business analyst specializing in executive communication.

Context:

- Source material [PASTE LONG DOCUMENT, REPORT, OR MEETING TRANSCRIPT]
- Target audience [C-SUITE/BOARD/TEAM LEADS]
- Decision context [WHAT DECISION THIS INFORMS]

Task:

- Compress the source into a one-page executive brief (max 400 words)
- Preserve all decision-critical information and discard supporting detail

- Include a “What changed” section if the source updates a prior version

Constraints:

- Do not add information not present in the source
- Maintain the original author’s conclusions — compress, do not reinterpret
- Structure as: Key Takeaway (one sentence), Context, Critical Findings, Recommended Action

Technique: *Context compression + fidelity constraints.*

A quality response might include: a tightly compressed brief that preserves every decision-critical point, no injected opinions, and a clear structure that enables rapid executive decision-making.

Your Prompt Hero Toolkit Doesn't End Here

The book gives you the frameworks. These four free bonuses give you the tools to apply them faster, go deeper, and keep growing long after the last chapter.

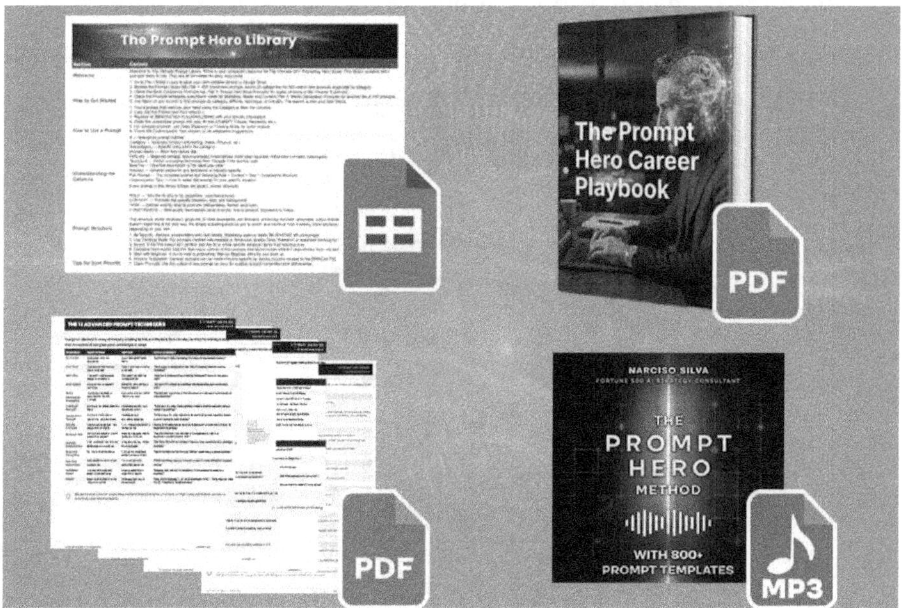

Sign up for free and get:

- **800+ ready-to-use business prompts library** organized by function, industry, and technique. For the days when you know what you need but can't find the right words, this library gives you a proven starting point in seconds instead of a blank screen.

- **Prompting for Career Growth, a 15,000-word standalone guide** with a complete system for turning your prompt skills into career advancement, from landing interviews to earning promotions.
- **The Reference Guides:** A set of cheat sheets with all the main topics of the book summarized for quick reference
- **The Audiobook:** so you can listen to the concepts of the book from anywhere.

You already invested in learning the method. These bonuses make sure you get the most out of it. **Free. Ten seconds. Scan the QR code or visit the link below.**

https://synecticpublishing.kit.com/7ba6afb204

Questions or feedback?
publishing@synecticstudio.com

CONCLUSION

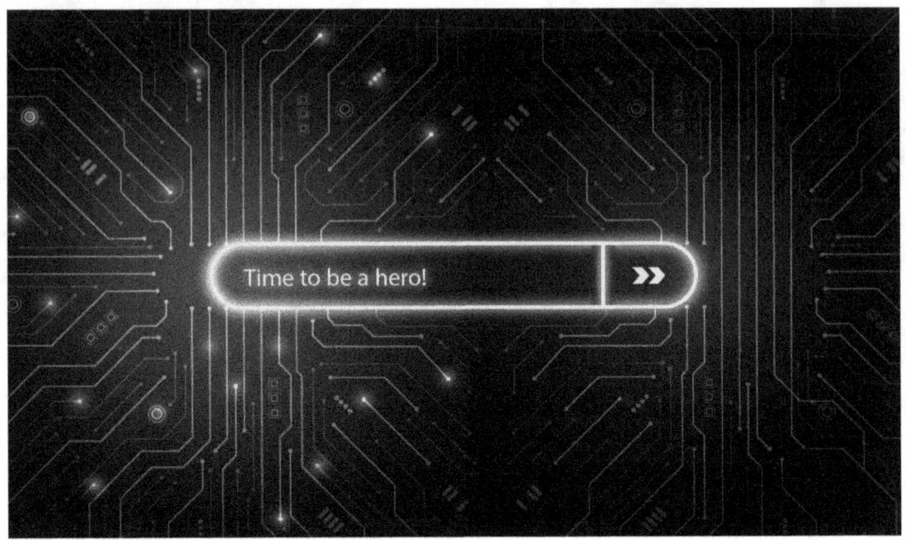

In an era where most professionals are endlessly chasing the next shiny AI tool, you've made a decision that sets you apart. You've chosen mastery over novelty. While others scramble to keep up with a constant stream of updates, platforms, and features, you've invested in something far more powerful and durable, which is the ability to think clearly, communicate intent precisely, and direct AI systems with confidence.

The true advantage in the age of AI doesn't belong to those who know the most tools but to those who know how to use any tool well. You've learned that effective prompting isn't about memorizing commands or mastering a specific interface. It's about intent, clarity, and knowing what you want, why it matters, and how to articulate it in a way that produces meaningful results. That's a timeless skill that will remain valuable long after today's tools are replaced by tomorrow's.

Throughout this book, we've explored how AI can amplify the work professionals already do best. You've seen how it supports productivity, accelerates creativity, sharpens analysis, strengthens communication, and unlocks new forms of innovation. Tasks that once demanded entire teams, long timelines, or significant budgets can now be executed with speed and precision when guided by thoughtful prompts and sound judgment. The advantage comes not from automation alone but from direction.

More importantly, you've learned that prompting isn't a technical trick but a leadership discipline. It forces you to frame problems carefully, define outcomes clearly, and think in structured ways. The professionals who extract the most value from AI aren't those who delegate thinking to machines but those who use machines to extend their thinking. They remain accountable, apply judgment, and decide what matters and what doesn't.

This journey has also emphasized that power without responsibility is fragile. Sustainable success with AI depends on oversight, ethics, and trust. Fact-checking, bias awareness, human review, and clear governance are necessary to ensure that speed doesn't undermine credibility and that innovation strengthens rather than erodes trust. Leaders who understand this will always outperform those who chase shortcuts.

As you reach the end of this book, take a moment to recognize what you've gained. You now have the tools to build your own prompt library tailored to your role, your industry, and your goals. Over time, this personal prompting playbook will save you and your team countless hours, sharpen decision-making, and create a lasting competitive edge.

But this isn't the end of the journey. It's the beginning of a new way of working. The real value now comes from practice. Therefore, I urge you to experiment with the advanced techniques shared in this book, refine your prompts, and observe the outcomes. Learn what works for you, and clock it. Prompting is a living skill, and every iteration makes you more capable, more confident, and more effective.

It's inevitable that AI will continue to evolve at a rapid pace. What won't change is the value of clear intent, structured thinking, disciplined oversight, and purposeful creativity. Use AI with these principles, and it will continue to reward you.

If this book has helped you think differently, work smarter, or move faster, I'd be grateful if you could share your experience with other readers by leaving a review on Amazon or your preferred platform. Your feedback helps others discover this resource and begin their own journey.

I'm excited for what you'll build, create, and lead next. Here's to your continued growth—and to becoming not just a user of AI but a true prompting hero.

Did You Find This Book Valuable?

I'd Love to Hear from You!

Your feedback makes a world of difference, not only to me as a new author, but also to other people seeking to unlock the value of AI in their lives.

If this book brought you insights, inspiration, or important information, would you have just 2 minutes to spare to share your thoughts?

Your review helps me create even better resources for you and helps others discover this valuable guide.

Whether it's a quick note or a detailed response, every piece of feedback counts and is deeply appreciated.

Thank you for supporting this journey!

Questions? Drop a line here: publishing@synecticstudio.com

REFERENCES

Abdelmenem, M. (2025, December 12). *A single Google search blew up Deloitte's $290,000 AI report*. Medium. https://pub.towardsai.net/one-professors-google-search-exposed-deloitte-s-290-000-ai-report-97d5e57dd8e0

Academic English Now. (2025, February 26). 5 *unbelievably useful AI tools for research in* 2025 (*better than ChatGPT*) [Video]. YouTube. https://www.youtube.com/watch?v=wmQVdzBRnN4

AI demystified: Introduction to large language models. (2024, December 13). Stanford University IT. https://uit.stanford.edu/service/techtraining/ai-demystified/llm

Akansha. (2024, October 21). Prompt chaining vs chain of thoughts CoT. *YourGPT.* https://yourgpt.ai/blog/general/prompt-chaining-vs-chain-of-thoughts

Akash, A. (2025, April 3). How to write product descriptions that sell like crazy. *Skill Arbitrage Blog.* https://skillarbitra.ge/blog/product-descriptions-that-sell-like-crazy/

Akolo, W. (2023, August 7). *Google Ads landing page examples: Designs for higher conversion*. HostAdvice. https://hostadvice.com/blog/digital-marketing/ppc/google-ads-landing-page-examples/

Alex. (2025, December 23). *AI writing prompts to create compelling copy for ads blogs and social media*. Pressmaster.ai. https://www.pressmaster.ai/article/ai-writing-prompts-create-compelling-copy-ads-blogs-social-media

Al Sawi, I., & Alaa, A. (2024). Navigating the impact: A study of editors' and proofreaders' perceptions of AI tools in editing and proofreading. *Discover Artificial Intelligence,* 4(1), 23. https://doi.org/10.1007/s44163-024-00116-5

Anand, B. N. (2008, January). *The value of a broader product portfolio.* Harvard Business Review. https://hbr.org/2008/01/the-value-of-a-broader-product-portfolio

Atieh, A. A., Hussein, A. A., Al-Jaghoub, S., Alheet, A. F., & Attiany, M. (2025). The impact of digital technology, automation, and data integration on supply chain performance: Exploring the moderating role of digital transformation. *Logistics,* 9(1), 11. https://doi.org/10.3390/logistics9010011

Aziz, M. (2026, January 8). I tested the top 10 AI scheduling assistants in 2026 (+reviews). *Lindy.* https://www.lindy.ai/blog/ai-scheduling-assistant

Bhairav, S. (2025, March 29). *Explaining types of prompt engineering.* Metric Coders. https://www.metriccoders.com/post/explaining-types-of-prompt-engineering

Bhatia, R. (2025, December 18). 8 best AI video repurposing tools for podcasters: 2026 edition. *Quso.ai.* https://quso.ai/blog/best-video-repurposing-tools-for-podcasters

Bogore, E. (2023, November 16). *How Morning Brew makes $13m from email marketing.* Encharge. https://encharge.io/how-morning-brew-makes-13m-from-email-marketing/

Bough, V., Ehrlich, O., Fanderl, H., & Schiff, R. (2023, March 23). *Experience-led growth: A new way to create value.* McKinsey. https://www.mckinsey.com/capabilities/growth-marketing-and-sales/our-insights/experience-led-growth-a-new-way-to-create-value

Brodsky, S. (2023, September 28). *Google DeepMind: Being more human to AI makes it perform better.* AI Business. https://aibusiness.com/nlp/to-make-ai-perform-better-researchers-turn-to-human-style-prompts

Bussey, S. (2025, January 22). The role of domain knowledge in effective prompt engineering. *Andovar.* https://blog.andovar.com/the-role-of-domain-knowledge-in-effective-prompt-engineering

Butler, J., Jaffe, S., Baym, N., Czerwinski, M., Iqbal, S., Nowak, K., Rintel, S., Sellen, A., Vorvoreanu, M., Abdulhamid, N. G., Amores,

J., Andersen, R., Awori, K., Axmed, M., Boyd, D., Brand, J., Buscher, G., Carignan, D., Chan, M., ... Teevan, J. (2023, December). *Microsoft new future of work report* 2023. Microsoft. https://www.microsoft.com/en-us/research/publication/microsoft-new-future-of-work-report-2023/

Buzdugan, S. (2025, May 7). *Day 48/100: Large language models (LLMs): The engines behind modern AI.* Medium. https://medium.com/@sebuzdugan/day-48-100-large-language-models-llms-the-engines-behind-modern-ai-ecf0fe495c35

Case studies: Brands already using generative ai for video ads (and lessons learned). (n.d.). Picasso Multimedia. https://picassomultimedia.com/blog-brands-using-generative-ai-for-video-ads-case-studies/

Castro, A. (2024, October 8). *How social selling is transforming sales in the digital age.* LinkedIn. https://www.linkedin.com/pulse/how-social-selling-transforming-sales-digital-age-alan-castro-luu3f/

Chaffey, D. (2016, June 22). *Introducing ecommerce success mapping.* Smart Insights. https://www.smartinsights.com/ecommerce/ecommerce-strategy/ecommerce-success-mapping/

Chaffey, D. (2020, October 1). *Pareto's 80:20 rule in marketing.* Smart Insights. https://www.smartinsights.com/marketing-planning/marketing-models/paretos-8020-rule-marketing/

The ChatGPT business toolkit: Copy-and-paste prompts for every department. (n.d.). LearnPrompt. https://learnprompt.org/chat-gpt-prompts-for-business/

Chechique, E. (@Edward Chechique). (2025, February 16). 10 *prompt mistakes you're making (and how to write AI prompts that work)* [Video]. YouTube. https://www.youtube.com/watch?v=jsf382WvH5I

Chen, W., Wang, X., Cohen, W. W., & Ma, X. (2024, September 17). Program of thoughts prompting: Disentangling computation from reasoning for numerical reasoning tasks. *Transactions on Machine Learning Research*. https://openreview.net/forum?id=YfZ4ZPt8zd

Chui, M., Hazan, E., Roberts, R., Singla, A., Smaje, K., Sukharevsky, A., Yee, L., & Zemmel, R. (2023, June 14). *The economic potential of generative AI: The next productivity frontier*. McKinsey & Company. https://www.mckinsey.com/capabilities/tech-and-ai/our-insights/the-economic-potential-of-generative-ai-the-next-productivity-frontier

Chui, M., Manyika, J., Bughin, J., Dobbs, R., Roxburgh, C., Sarrazin, H., Sands, G., & Westergren, M. (2012, July 1). *The social economy: Unlocking value and productivity through social technologies*. McKinsey & Company. https://www.mckinsey.com/industries/technology-media-and-telecommunications/our-insights/the-social-economy

Cintra, J. (2025, July 16). *Meta ad formats in 2025: Your quick guide to picking the right one*. Dataslayer. https://www.dataslayer.ai/blog/meta-ad-formats-in-2025-guide

Cleary, D. (2025, August 12). Program of thoughts prompting guide. *PromptHub*. https://www.prompthub.us/blog/program-of-thoughts-prompting-guide

Connell, A. (2026, January 15). 13 *best social media scheduling tools* (2026 *pros and cons*). Adam Connell. https://adamconnell.me/social-media-scheduler-tools/

Cook, J. (2023, June 28). *How to write effective prompts for ChatGPT: 7 essential steps for best results*. Forbes. https://www.forbes.com/sites/jodiecook/2023/06/26/how-to-write-effective-prompts-for-chatgpt-7-essential-steps-for-best-results/

Curry, D. (2026, January 7). *ChatGPT revenue and usage statistics* (2026). Business of Apps. https://www.businessofapps.com/data/chatgpt-statistics/

The Daily Sales. (2024, August 9). 12 *B2B social selling statistics for* 2024. LinkedIn. https://www.linkedin.com/pulse/12-b2b-social-selling-statistics-2024-the-daily-sales-suzhe/

Dobariya, P. (2025, April 25). *Data visualization in financial services providing the visual edge beyond numbers.* GetOnData. https://getondata.com/data-visualization-in-financial-services

Drain, G. (2025, November 7). 75% of consumers judge a company's credibility by its website. *Made for Web.* https://madeforweb.co.uk/blog/75-of-consumers-judge-a-companys-credibility-by-its-website

Eastwood, B. (2025, October 6). *AI implementation strategies*: 4 *insights from MIT Sloan Management Review.* MIT Sloan. https://mitsloan.mit.edu/ideas-made-to-matter/ai-implementation-strategies-4-insights-mit-sloan-management-review

Edelman. (2025). 2025 *Edelman trust barometer*: *Special report*: *Brand Trust, From We to Me.* https://www.edelman.com/trust/2025/trust-barometer/special-report-brands

The 80/20 *rule*: *How to streamline workplace culture for maximum impact.* (2025, January 2). InitiativeOne. https://www.initiativeone.com/post/the-80-20-rule-how-to-streamline-workplace-culture-for-maximum-impact

Ellis, C., & Evans, C. (2025, April 30). Email marketing ROI: Average return on email marketing. *EmailToolTester.* https://www.emailtooltester.com/en/blog/email-marketing-roi/

Elwyn, J. (2026, January 9). *The best AI video generator* 2026: *An updated comparison of* 10 *tools.* MASV. https://massive.io/gear-guides/the-best-ai-video-generator-comparison/

Epstein, R. (1992). Can machines think? *AI Magazine,* 13(2), 80–95. https://ojs.aaai.org/aimagazine/index.php/aimagazine/article/download/993/911

Fay, O. (2022, May 6). *Value of #1 position on Google for traffic: Positional analysis study* [2023]. Poll the People. https://pollthepeople.app/the-value-of-google-result-positioning-3/

Finn, T., & Downie, A. (n.d.). *Agentic AI vs. generative AI.* IBM. https://www.ibm.com/think/topics/agentic-ai-vs-generative-ai

Gallo, A. (2014, October 29). *The value of keeping the right customers.* Harvard Business Review. https://hbr.org/2014/10/the-value-of-keeping-the-right-customers

Generative AI could raise global GDP by 7%. (2023, April 5). Goldman Sachs. https://www.goldmansachs.com/insights/articles/generative-ai-could-raise-global-gdp-by-7-percent

Gewirtz, D. (2025, January 15). *The five biggest mistakes people make when prompting an AI.* ZDNET. https://www.zdnet.com/article/the-five-biggest-mistakes-people-make-when-prompting-an-ai/

God of Prompt. (2026, January 19). Common AI prompt mistakes and how to fix them. *God of Prompt.* https://www.godofprompt.ai/blog/common-ai-prompt-mistakes-and-how-to-fix-them

Goldenfein, J., & Yang, F. (2025, August 14). *Does AI really boost productivity at work? Research shows gains don't come cheap or easy.* The Conversation. https://theconversation.com/does-ai-really-boost-productivity-at-work-research-shows-gains-dont-come-cheap-or-easy-263127

Gratton, L. (2024, August 14). *Seven truths about hybrid work and productivity.* MIT Sloan Management Review. https://sloanreview.mit.edu/article/seven-truths-about-hybrid-work-and-productivity/

Guinness, H. (2025, October 9). The best AI image generators in 2026. *Zapier.* https://zapier.com/blog/best-ai-image-generator/

Gunner, J. (2022, July 6). *List of all 50 US state abbreviations.* Your Dictionary. https://www.yourdictionary.com/articles/state-abbreviations

Hada, R. (2024, December 12). LLM vs GPT: Understanding key differences and applications. *Future AGI.* https://futureagi.com/blogs/llm-vs-gpt

Holliday, C. (2025, June 19). *Lessons from Edelman's Brand Trust report.* Creative Salon. https://creative.salon/articles/features/edelman-brand-trust-report-2025

Hott, A., & Taheer, F. (2025, November 25). 40+ *email marketing statistics you need to know for* 2026. OptinMonster. https://optinmonster.com/email-marketing-statistics/

Huang, B. (2024, August 23). *How to measure and predict ROI for your content marketing strategy.* Clearscope. https://www.clearscope.io/blog/content-marketing-roi

Ikram, A. (2024, January 30). Key cybersecurity compliance standards: HIPAA, GDPR, PCI DSS. *PureDome.* https://www.puredome.com/blog/intro-to-key-cybersecurity-compliance-standards

Ionita, O. (2025, December 24). Crafting your SEO strategy: A step-by-step guide. *CRO Benchmark.* https://www.crobenchmark.com/blog/seo-strategy-guide-4e65884c

Jerenz, A., Storozhev, A., D'Aversa, L., Boksha, N., Khan, N., Jogani, R., & Ivanov, A. (2024, November 27). *How high performers optimize IT productivity for revenue growth: A leader's guide.* McKinsey & Company. https://www.mckinsey.com/capabilities/tech-and-ai/our-insights/how-high-performers-optimize-it-productivity-for-revenue-growth-a-leaders-guide

Jin. (2025, May 27). *The impact of AI-augmented tools on web development: Enhancing productivity, design, and code quality - software testing and development company.* ShiftAsia. https://shiftasia.com/column/the-impact-of-ai-augmented-tools-on-web-development-enhancing-productivity-design-and-code-quality/

Kaput, M. (2025, November 21). New McKinsey report shows mostly experimentation, not transformation, with AI so far. *Marketing AI Institute*. https://www.marketingaiinstitute.com/blog/mckinsey-report-finds-few-ai-innovators

Kellton. (2025, September 19). Communicating with AI: Prompt engineering strategies every leader should know. *Kellton*. https://www.kellton.com/kellton-tech-blog/prompt-engineering-for-business-in-their-ai-decision-making

Lacy, L. (2024, September 13). *OpenAI: Everything you need to know about the company that started a generative AI revolution*. CNET. https://www.cnet.com/tech/services-and-software/openai-everything-you-need-to-know-about-the-company-that-started-a-generative-ai-revolution/

Laoudai, O. (2025, October 30). *Prompt engineering: Techniques, examples & best practices guide*. Infomineo. https://infomineo.com/artificial-intelligence/prompt-engineering-techniques-examples-best-practices-guide/

Laurent, A. (2026, January 2). *What is context engineering? A guide for AI & LLMs*. IntuitionLabs. https://intuitionlabs.ai/articles/what-is-context-engineering

Lessons from Adobe's shift to subscriptions: A pricing transformation story. (2025, May 21). Monetizely. https://www.getmonetizely.com/articles/lessons-from-adobes-shift-to-subscriptions-a-pricing-transformation-story

LinkedIn. (n.d.). *Social selling: Definition, benefits & tips for sales leaders*. https://business.linkedin.com/sales-solutions/social-selling

Litan, A. (2025, October 6). *Context engineering is the new prompt engineering*. Gartner. https://www.gartner.com/en/articles/context-engineering

The London School of Economics and Political Science. (2024, October 25). *More than a third of business meetings are unproductive due to a lack of generational diversity.* https://www.lse.ac.uk/news/latest-news-from-lse/j-october-2024/more-than-a-third-of-business-meetings-are-unproductive-due-to-a-lack-of-generational-diversity

Matt. (2025, May 31). How to repurpose social media content 2026: 20 smart strategies that boost engagement by 300% (save 60% time). *SocialRails.* https://socialrails.com/blog/repurpose-social-media-content

Meabe, C. (2024, August 2). *TAM, SAM, SOM: How to calculate them for your industry.* Foundation. https://foundationinc.co/lab/tam-sam-som

Miguelañez, C. (2025, January 30). Iterative prompt refinement: Step-by-step guide. *Latitude.* https://latitude-blog.ghost.io/blog/iterative-prompt-refinement-step-by-step-guide/

Mike, M. (@Matt Mike). (2025, September 30). *I tested 53 AI tools for data analysis: These 5 are the best* [Video]. YouTube. https://www.youtube.com/watch?v=RYTjU_x6fAQ

MVC. (2025, February 18). *The psychology of pricing.* Market Value Creation. https://www.mvcorg.com/the-psychology-of-pricing/

Newmark, W. (2025, November 12). *Data brokers and data privacy: Monetization, regulation, and how they affect consumers.* Usercentrics. https://usercentrics.com/knowledge-hub/data-brokers-and-data-privacy-monetization/

Pavitra M. (2026, January 19). *AI negative prompt examples for better content output.* ClickUp. https://clickup.com/blog/ai-negative-prompt-examples/

Piccolo, V. (n.d.). *LLM vs chatbot in 2025.* Callin.io. https://callin.io/llm-vs-chatbot/

Pozen, R. C., & Fry, R. (2025, October 15). *For AI productivity gains, let team leaders write the rules.* MIT Sloan Management Review. https://sloanreview.mit.edu/article/for-ai-productivity-gains-let-team-leaders-write-the-rules/

The principles and practices of prompt engineering. (2025, November 22). *Prompts.ai.* https://www.prompts.ai/en/blog/the-principles-and-practices-of-prompt-engineering

Prompt design strategies. (n.d.). Google AI for Developers. https://ai.google.dev/gemini-api/docs/prompting-strategies

PwC. (2025, June 3). *The fearless future*: 2025 *global AI jobs barometer.* https://www.pwc.com/gx/en/services/ai/ai-jobs-barometer.html

Ramlochan, S. (2024, June 9). *Comprehensive and simplified lifecycles for effective AI prompt management.* Prompt Engineering & AI Institute. https://promptengineering.org/comprehensive-and-simplified-lifecycles-for-effective-ai-prompt-management/

Redlim Group. (2025, August 17). *Best AI tools for meetings and note-taking in* 2025. REDLIMOO. https://redlimoo.com/ai/best-ai-tools-for-meetings-and-note-taking-in-2025/

Redmond, S. (2023, March 25). *LLM prompt engineering patterns.* LinkedIn. https://www.linkedin.com/pulse/llm-prompt-engineering-patterns-stephen-redmond/

Reichheld, F. (2001). *Prescription for cutting costs.* Bain & Company. https://media.bain.com/Images/BB_Prescription_cutting_costs.pdf

Rosner, C. (n.d.). *Show me that you know me.* TTEC. https://www.ttec.com/articles/show-me-you-know-me

Saji, L. (2025, December 2). *How to automate repetitive tasks & reclaim your team's time.* Nimble. https://www.nimblework.com/blog/automate-repetitive-tasks

Sawaya, A., Wang, K. W., Bu, L., & Chang, M. (2025, November 28). *Beyond the hype*: *Unlocking value from the AI revolution.* McKinsey

& Company. https://www.mckinsey.com/cn/our-insights/our-insights/beyond-the-hype-unlocking-value-from-the-ai-revolution

Schema-first prompting strategies. (2025, October 11). Emergent Mind. https://www.emergentmind.com/topics/schema-first-prompting

Schor, J. B. (2025, May 22). *The surprising viability of the four-day workweek*. MIT Sloan Management Review. https://sloanreview.mit.edu/article/the-surprising-viability-of-the-four-day-workweek/

Schulhoff, S. (2024, October 23). *Prompt engineering guide*. Learn Prompting. https://learnprompting.org/docs/introduction

Schulhoff, S. (2025, March 6). *Technique #1: Instructions in prompts*. Learn Prompting. https://learnprompting.org/docs/basics/instructions

Shah, D. (2025, March 1). Delimiters in prompt engineering. *Portkey. https://portkey.ai/blog/delimiters-in-prompt-engineering*

Shani, I., & GitHub Staff (2024, February 7). Survey reveals AI's impact on the developer experience. *GitHub*. https://github.blog/news-insights/research/survey-reveals-ais-impact-on-the-developer-experience/

Singh, T. (2025, January 3). *Advanced prompt engineering techniques for AI developers: Unlocking the power of LLMs*. Medium. https://pub.towardsai.net/advanced-prompt-engineering-techniques-for-ai-developers-unlocking-the-power-of-llms-7187883741c9

Singla, A., Sukharevsky, A., Yee, L., Chui, M., Hall, B., & Balakrishnan, T. (2025, November 5). *The state of AI in 2025: Agents, innovation, and transformation*. McKinsey & Company. https://www.mckinsey.com/capabilities/quantumblack/our-insights/the-state-of-ai

Somers, M. (2023, October 19). *How generative AI can boost highly skilled workers' productivity*. MIT Sloan School of Management. https://mitsloan.mit.edu/ideas-made-to-matter/how-generative-ai-can-boost-highly-skilled-workers-productivity

Soni, A. (n.d.). *Creating content pillars for social media: Step-by-step guide with examples.* StoryChief Insights. https://storychief.io/blog/social-media-content-pillars

Stanford Tech Training. (2024a, September 5). *LLMs for the non-technical (AI Simplified series)* [Video]. YouTube. https://www.youtube.com/watch?v=EQj9q_4dJ0k

Stanford Tech Training. (2024b, September 10). *How LLM learns: With Charlie the computer (AI Simplified series)* [Video]. YouTube. https://www.youtube.com/watch?v=tWpDKAZ8pVk

The state of enterprise AI. (2025, December 9). OpenAI. https://openai.com/index/the-state-of-enterprise-ai-2025-report/

Stryker, C., & Kavlakoglu, E. (n.d.). *What is artificial intelligence (AI)?* IBM. https://www.ibm.com/think/topics/artificial-intelligence

Tadros, E., & Karp, P. (2025, October 5). Deloitte to refund government, admits using AI in $440k report. *Australian Financial Review.* https://www.afr.com/companies/professional-services/deloitte-to-refund-government-after-admitting-ai-errors-in-440k-report-20251005-p5n05p

TAM, SAM & SOM: What do they mean & how do you calculate them? (2025, April 7). Engage Coders. https://www.engagecoders.com/tam-sam-som-what-do-they-mean-how-do-you-calculate-them/

Tardi, C. (2025, May 30). *The 80-20 rule (aka Pareto principle): What it is and how it works.* Investopedia. https://www.investopedia.com/terms/1/80-20-rule.asp

Taylor-Chadwick, H. (2024, April 30). Time management statistics: Understand where your workday goes. *Runn.* https://www.runn.io/blog/time-management-statistics

10 proven strategies for crafting effective B2B calls to action. (2024, December 30). *Intelemark.* https://www.intelemark.com/blog/10-proven-strategies-for-crafting-effective-b2b-calls-to-action/

Teter, B. (2025, October 28). Work meetings in numbers: Latest meeting statistics [2026]. *Archie*. https://archieapp.co/blog/meeting-statistics/

Thakur, T. (2025, July 15). *Generative AI statistics 2026: Tools, usage, market & ROI*. TechKV. https://techkv.com/generative-ai-statistics/

Timmermann, R. (2024, January 24). A data-driven guide to Google CTR by position in 2025. *Timmermann Group*. https://www.wearetg.com/blog/google-ctr-by-position/

Trinh, K., Seidenberger, S., Wijewickrama, R., Jadliwala, M., & Maiti, A. (2025). *A picture is worth a thousand prompts? Efficacy of iterative human-driven prompt refinement in image regeneration tasks*. ArXiv. https://arxiv.org/html/2504.20340v1

2025: *The year the frontier firm is born*. (2025, April 23). Microsoft. https://www.microsoft.com/en-us/worklab/work-trend-index/2025-the-year-the-frontier-firm-is-born

Up Inc. (2024, February 26). *Organic vs. PPC in 2024: Which is a better investment?* https://upinc.co/organic-vs-ppc-2024-ctr-results-best-practices/

Valchanov, I. (2025, July 13). 10 best AI brainstorming generators in 2026. *Juma*. https://juma.ai/blog/ai-brainstorming-generators

Ventura, L. (2024, April 18). *Unemployment rates around the world* 2024. Global Finance Magazine. https://gfmag.com/data/economic-data/world-unemployment-rates/

Widening gap between consumer expectations and reality in personalization signals warning for brands, Accenture interactive research finds. (2018, May 3). Accenture. https://newsroom.accenture.com/news/2018/widening-gap-between-consumer-expectations-and-reality-in-personalization-signals-warning-for-brands-accenture-interactive-research-finds

Winslow, G. (2025, October 23). *Spectrum Reach has deployed more than 15,000 AI-powered ad campaigns*. TV Tech. https://www.

tvtechnology.com/news/spectrum-reach-has-deployed-more-than-15-000-ai-powered-ad-campaigns

Wrótniak, K. (2025, June 10). *10 best AI coding assistant tools in 2025: Guide for developers*. Droids on Roids. https://www.thedroidsonroids.com/blog/best-ai-coding-assistant-tools

Yang, C., Wang, X., Lu, Y., Liu, H., Le, Q. V., Zhou, D., & Chen, X. (2023, September 6). *Large language models as optimizers*. ArXiv. https://doi.org/10.48550/arXiv.2309.03409

Zewe, A. (2025, November 26). *Researchers discover a shortcoming that makes LLMs less reliable*. MIT News, Massachusetts Institute of Technology. https://news.mit.edu/2025/shortcoming-makes-llms-less-reliable-1126

Image References

Altmann, G. (@Geralt). (2025, April 12). *Atom, physics, icon* [Image]. Pixabay. https://pixabay.com/illustrations/atom-physics-icon-science-9529721/

Ann H. (@Ann H). (2023, January 31). *Letters on dice* [Image]. Pexels. https://www.pexels.com/photo/letters-on-dice-15380267/

Blazek, L. (@Lukas Blazek). (2017, November 2). *Charts on black wooden table* [Image]. Pexels. https://www.pexels.com/photo/charts-on-black-wooden-table-669622/

Blomkvist, M. (@Mikael Blomkvist). (2021, January 12). *Person drawing on a notebook* [Image]. Pexels. https://www.pexels.com/photo/person-drawing-on-a-notebook-6476806/

Bui, T. (@Tao Bui). (2021, October 2). *A laptop computer sitting on top of a desk* [Image]. Unsplash. https://unsplash.com/photos/a-laptop-computer-sitting-on-top-of-a-desk-BjcyfRxpdfQ

CarlosOlmos. (2025, June 11). Prompt: *Blue futuristic technological science fiction and technology background.* [AI-generated Image]. Pixabay. https://pixabay.com/illustrations/ai-generated-robot-technology-9654445/

cottonbro studio. (2021, February 12). *Sticky notes on the task board wall.* [Image]. Pexels. https://www.pexels.com/photo/sticky-notes-on-the-task-board-wall-6804093/

Dantès, E. (@Edmond Dantès). (2021, June 30). *Woman giving a presentation at a business meeting.* [Image]. Pexels. https://www.pexels.com/photo/woman-giving-a-presentation-at-a-business-meeting-8555768/

Dziuba, T. (@Tobias Dziuba). (2018, March 15). *Scribbled notes on a computer keyboard* [Image]. Pexels. https://www.pexels.com/photo/scribbled-notes-on-a-computer-keyboard-942331/

fauxels. (2019, November 5). *Person using a laptop* [Image]. Pexels. https://www.pexels.com/photo/person-using-a-laptop-3183131/

Fischer, M. (@Max Fischer). (2020, November 13). *Close-up shot of discount tags.* [Image]. Pexels. https://www.pexels.com/photo/close-up-shot-of-discount-tags-5872174/

Grace, H. (@hannah grace). (2019, April 18). *A white box with writing on it next to a plant* [Image]. Unsplash. https://unsplash.com/photos/a-white-box-with-writing-on-it-next-to-a-plant-j9JoYpaJH3A?

Hassan, M. (@Mohamed_hassan). (2024, September 4). *Scholarship education student* [Image]. Pixabay. https://pixabay.com/vectors/scholarship-education-student-9013565/

Miroshnichenko, T. (@Tima Miroshnichenko). (2021, February 22). 3 *women sitting at the table* [Image]. Pexels. https://www.pexels.com/photo/3-women-sitting-at-the-table-6913241/

Mishra, S. (Sanket Mishra). (2023, May 1). *Webpage of ChatGPT, a prototype AI chatbot, is seen on the website of OpenAI, on a smartphone. Examples, capabilities, and limitations are shown* [Image]. Pexels.

https://www.pexels.com/photo/webpage-of-chatgpt-a-prototype-ai-chatbot-is-seen-on-the-website-of-openai-on-a-smartphone-examples-capabilities-and-limitations-are-shown-16629368/

Nilov, M. (@Mikhail Nilov). (2021, August 19). *Woman and man in goggles sitting by table and working on electronics* [Image]. Pexels. https://www.pexels.com/photo/woman-and-man-in-goggles-sitting-by-table-and-working-on-electronics-9242849/

Ribkhan, M. (@ribkhan). (2018, March 25). *Email, newsletter, email marketing* [Image]. Pixabay. https://pixabay.com/vectors/email-newsletter-email-marketing-3249062/

Seymour, A. (@popmelon). (2024, March 14). Prompt: *Idea, light* [AI-generated Image]. Pixabay. https://pixabay.com/illustrations/ai-generated-idea-light-lightbulb-8630991/

Xəlfəquliyev, T. (@Tahir Xəlfəquliyev). (2025, August 1). *Children engaged in creative art activity indoors* [Image]. Pexels. https://www.pexels.com/photo/children-engaged-in-creative-art-activity-indoors-33738065/

Zaric, M. (@Marija Zaric). (2021, November 12). *A group of people walking up some steps* [Image]. Unsplash. https://unsplash.com/photos/a-group-of-people-walking-up-some-steps-ZyiAmD17-6M

www.ingramcontent.com/pod-product-compliance
Lightning Source LLC
LaVergne TN
LVHW010649110826
845149LV00014B/3000